Targeting PHONICS

★ Book 3 ★

This book belongs to

....

....

Targeting Phonics Book 3

Reprinted 2023

ISBN: 978-1-92572-636-7

Published by Pascal Press
PO Box 250
Glebe NSW 2037
www.pascalpress.com.au
contact@pascalpress.com.au

Design: Janice Bowles
Author: Norah Colvin
Publisher: Lynn Dickinson
Typesetter: BSMART Publishing
Illustrator: Paul Lennon
Printed by Vivar Printing/Green Giant Press

Contents

⋆ Phonics explained ⋆

Phonics helps children **decode** words for reading and **encode** words for spelling. **Decoding** requires them to see the letters, match them with a sound and blend the sounds together to say the word. **Encoding** requires them to hear the sounds in a word and match each sound with a corresponding letter or combination of letters. The ability to decode and encode words efficiently underpins success with reading and writing.

The *Targeting Phonics* series uses a systematic synthetic phonics approach with reference to the progression recommended in the Australian Curriculum. It introduces students to the 26 letters of the alphabet (graphemes) and their relationship to the 44 sounds (phonemes) of the English language, which the letters represent.

The Synthetic Phonics approach encourages children to listen to all the phonemes (individual sounds) and blend them, or 'synthesise' them, to form words, such as 'b' + 'a' + 't' = bat. Reading and spelling are taught in relationship to each other — if you can read a word, you can spell it. Writing the words also helps to consolidate this learning and is included in every unit.

Prior to the Synthetic Phonics methodology, schools often used Analytic phonics, where children were encouraged to identify the sound of the first letter and guess the rest of the word using rhymes or word-building strategies such as onset and rime. Reading and spelling were taught as separate skills, rather than being integrated.

⋆ About the author ⋆

Norah Colvin is a teacher with over 20 years' experience in early childhood classrooms. She is passionate about literacy education and enjoys sharing children's first steps into literacy. She has also supported learners who experienced difficulty attaining literacy skills the first time round.

⋆ How to use this book ⋆

On completing Book 3, students will have been introduced to the most common sounds and their representation in the English language. They should be able to decode single and multi-syllable words they encounter.

Photocopiable lists of decodable words for Units 1—3 and 6—7 are in the back of the book. The word lists for each vowel digraph and trigraph include the most common spelling and alternate spellings. The Units cover:

- 'r' controlled vowels: ar, er, or
- vowel digraphs: ow, oi
- vowel trigraphs: ear, air
- consonant trigraphs: tch, dge
- three-letter consonant blends: scr, str, spr, spl
- consonant digraph blends: shr, thr
- decoding and spelling words with two or more syllables, including compound words
- adding endings to verbs to create word families and to create comparative adjectives
- silent letters and less common sounds

Four photographs introduce each sound. As with Books 1 and 2, these Sound Cards can be accessed online using the QR code on the page, for an image and audio pronunciation of the sound. Students should watch and listen to the Sound Card before completing the activity. **Note:** the syllable lessons do not have Sound Cards.

Revision activities follow each unit and include reading comprehension to provide additional practice of the unit activities. **The Assessment** section at the end of the book covers all Units.

Read and Spell

Students' growing knowledge of how sounds (phonemes) are represented by individual letters and combinations of letters (graphemes) enables them to learn to read and spell an increasing number of decodable words, including words having two or more syllables.

Students read and write words using various ways of spelling phonemes and learn to choose the correct way of representing the phonemes in different words.

High Frequency Words

Students learn to recognise by sight many high frequency words in Units 1 to 4, and lists of these are included in the back of the book. On completion of Book 3, students will know over 200 high frequency words and will be able to decode most others they encounter.

Comprehension

Students read short passages formed using decodable and known high frequency words to practise reading and comprehension.

It is suggested that students proceed through the book, completing the lessons in sequence. This will ensure that all words encountered in activities are ones that students have already learned to decode or recognise as high frequency words.

⋆ Version 9.0 Australian Curriculum correlations ⋆

Targeting Phonics Book 3 introduces students to the long vowel digraphs not covered in Book 2. In addition students will:

- Understand that words are units of meaning and can be made of more than one meaningful part (AC9EFLY15)
- Recognise and know how to use grammatical morphemes to create word families (AC9E1LY15)
- Segment words into separate phonemes (sounds) including consonant blends or clusters at the beginnings and ends of words (phonological awareness) (AC9E1LY09)
- Use short vowels, common long vowels, consonant blends and digraphs to write words, and blend these to read one- and two-syllable words (AC9E1LY11)
- Understand that a letter can represent more than one sound and that a syllable must contain a vowel sound (AC9E1LY12)
- Use phoneme–grapheme (sound–letter/s) matches, including vowel digraphs, less common long vowel patterns, consonant clusters and silent letters when reading and writing words of one or more syllables, including compound words (AC9E2LY10)
- Manipulate more complex sounds in spoken words and use knowledge of blending, segmenting, phoneme deletion and phoneme substitution to read and write words (AC9E2LY09)
- Spell one- and two-syllable words with common letter patterns (AC9E1LY13)
- Read and write an increasing number of high frequency words (AC9E1LY14)
- Segment words into separate phonemes (sounds) including consonant blends or clusters at the beginnings and ends of words (phonological awareness) (AC9E1LY09)
- Use short vowels, common long vowels, consonant blends and digraphs to write words, and blend these to read one- and two-syllable words (AC9E1LY11)
- Use comprehension strategies such as visualising, predicting, connecting, summarising, monitoring and questioning to build literal and inferred meaning (AC9E2LY05)
- Write words legibly and with growing fluency using unjoined upper-case and lower-case letters (AC9E2LY08)
- Build morphemic word families using knowledge of prefixes and suffixes (AC9E2LY12)

⋆ Glossary ⋆

Adjective	a word that describes a noun
Analytic Phonics	Analytic Phonics starts with a word and takes it apart to identify its parts, for example: 'bat' = 'b' + 'at'
Compound words	words that are formed by joining two smaller words together
Consonants	consonants are produced when the air is restricted in some way; in English there are 24 consonant sounds, most of which are represented by one letter and some which are represented by two letters, such as 'sh' and 'ch'
Decode	see the letters, match them with a sound and blend the sounds together to say the word
Digraph	a combination of two letters representing one sound, for example 'sh' as in 'shoe', 'ch' as in 'church', 'th' as in 'thimble' or 'there', 'oa' as in 'boat' or 'ea' as in 'peach'
Encode	listen to the sounds in a word and write the corresponding letter or combination of letters to match each sound
Graphemes	letters used to represent the sounds of the language
Irregular verbs	a verb in which the past tense does not follow the regular '-ed' pattern
Long vowels	vowel sounds that are long in duration
Noun	the name of a person, place or thing
Phonemes	individual units of sound heard in the language
Phonics	the relationships between graphemes and phonemes; understanding how letters and groups of letters are used to represent the sounds of the language
Phonemic awareness	the ability to hear and manipulate different sounds in words
Prefix	a letter or group of letters added to the beginning of a word to change its meaning or function
Quadgraphs	four letters used to represent one sound, for example: 'eigh' as in 'eight' or 'weight'
Regular verb	a verb in which the past tense follows the usual 'ed' pattern
Schwa sound	the vowel in an unstressed syllable usually has the schwa sound
Short vowels	vowel sounds that are short in duration and cannot be lengthened without distortion
Split digraph	when the two letters that represent one sound are split by another letter, for example ae as in 'cake'
Suffix	a letter or group of letters added to the end of a word to change its meaning or function
Syllable	a letter or group of letters that contains a vowel and makes up a word or part of a word, usually having one beat, for example: 'bell' has one vowel sound and one beat, it has one syllable; 'ribbon' has two separate vowel sounds and two beats, it has two syllables
Synthetic phonics	Synthetic Phonics starts with individual sounds and blends them together to form words, for example: 'b' + 'a' + 't' = 'bat'
Trigraphs	three letters used to represent one sound, for example: 'igh' as in 'high' or 'light'
Unvoiced consonants	consonants that are made without the use of the vocal cords
Verb	a process, an action, or a being word. Every sentence has a verb.
Voiced consonants	consonants that are made with the use of the vocal cords
Vowels	sounds formed without obstruction to the flow of air by the tongue, teeth or lips; usually represented by the letters 'a', 'e', 'i', 'o', and 'u', either individually or in combination; the letters are sometimes combined with 'y' as in 'boy' or 'w' as in 'cow'; a vowel is necessary in every word and syllable in the English language.

⋆ Revision of Book 1 and 2 ⋆

In Book 1, we learned all letters of the alphabet and their most common sounds.
In Book 2, we learned the common long vowel sounds and common consonant digraphs. We learned that some letters represent more than one sound and that there are different ways of spelling the same sound
In both books, we blended the sounds to read words and listened to sounds in words to spell them. We also learned to recognise some high frequency words by sight.
The following exercises provide practise with what was learned in Books 1 and 2 before we go on to new work.

Decoding

Read the words. Draw lines to match them to the pictures.

cake
bike
shop
chop
bench
mole
mule
moth
sheep

peach
fly
wheel
bow
dice
moose
cage
book
moon

  ISBN: 9781925726367

Spelling

Say the names of the pictures below. Stretch out the word to hear the sounds at the beginning, in the middle and at the end.
Write the words on the lines below. Remember, there are different ways to spell the sounds.

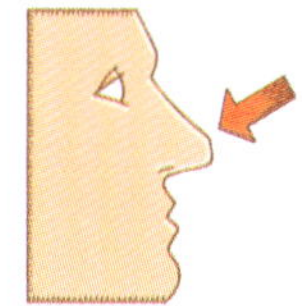

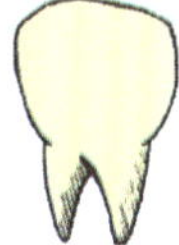

High frequency words

In Book 2, you learned these high frequency words.
Colour the words you know. Practise the ones you need to learn.

your	day	play	his	her
all	their	after	she	came
walk	by	be	stay	water
brother	sister	out	please	saw
as	put	who	whole	what
guy	buy	can't	new	our
friend	school	near	goes	could
should	would			

  ISBN: 9781925726367

Comprehension

Read the sentences. Draw a picture to match.

The cook made a peach pie for lunch. The children ate it all up real quick.	In the night when the moon was bright, the boys and girls could play by the pool.

We saw a moose in a cage at the zoo. It was a big moose. It did not drink fruit juice. It drank water.	Eight big sheep ate all the green grass. They drank all the water. They left no grass and no water for the six little goats.

  ISBN: 9781925726367

Comprehension

Look at the pictures. Read the sentences. Write in the missing word.

I saw a

___ ___ ___ ___ ___

ship zoom by the moon.

The ___ ___ ___ ___

and the queen gave some cake to the good children.

We went to the

___ ___ ___ ___ ___

and swam in the water.

This sentence is jumbled. Write it correctly on the lines below.

children The like chase school. play to at

  ISBN: 9781925726367

r controlled vowel sound  as in *star*

Use this QR code to watch and listen to the **letter AR** sound cards below

 star	 car
 shark	 farm

There are different ways to spell the **ar** sound as in star.
These words also have the **ar** sound.
Look at the pictures. Read the words. See the part that spells the **ar** sound.

	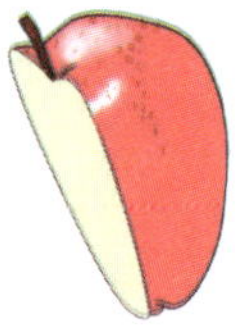			
giraffe	half	heart	grass	laugh

  ISBN: 9781925726367

r controlled vowel sound ar as in *star*

Each of these words has the ‘ar’ sound as in ‘star’. Read the words. Underline or highlight the letters that spell the ‘ar’ sound.

ar	car	star	far	tart
mart	part	mark	shark	barn
farm	arm	bar	jar	start
park	sharp	scarf	chart	yard
laugh	heart	half	grass	giraffe
fast	past	glass		

Read the words. Draw lines to match them to the pictures.

Choose a word with the **ar** sound from the boxes above to complete these sentences.

1. I had a ____ ____ ____ ____ ____ of milk with my lunch.
2. Mum cut the cake in ____ ____ ____ ____ for my brother and me.
3. The red car went ____ ____ ____ ____ down the road.
4. We went ____ ____ ____ ____ a farm on our way to the beach.
5. The little boy cut his arm on a ____ ____ ____ ____ ____ stick.
6. My dad makes me ____ ____ ____ ____ ____ when he tells me jokes.

  ISBN: 9781925726367

r controlled vowel sound  as in *fern*

Use this QR code to watch and listen to the **letter ER** sound cards below

 fern	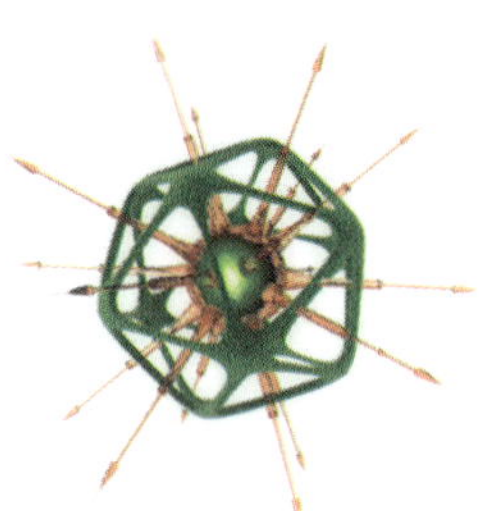 germ
 kerb	 her

There are different ways to spell the **er** sound as in fern.
These words also have the **er** sound.
Look at the pictures. Read the words. See the part that spells the **er** sound.

			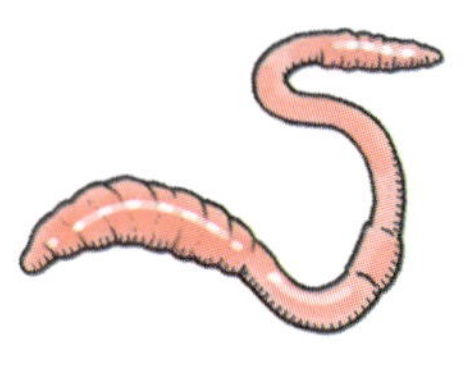	
bird	surf	nurse	worm	pearl

  ISBN: 9781925726367

r controlled vowel sound er as in *fern*

Each of these words has the 'er' sound as in 'fern'. Read the words. Underline or highlight the letters that spell the 'er' sound.

er	fern	her	kerb	perch
verb	term	herd	herb	germ
verse	nerve	serve		
bird	fir	first	stir	twirl
shirt	skirt	dirt	squirt	girl
surf	turf	hurt	curl	turn
burn	church	fur	burst	nurse
purse	curve			
word	world	worth	work	worm
earn	search	pearl	earth	
learn	heard	were		

Read the words. Draw lines to match them to the pictures.

Choose a word with the *er* sound from the boxes above to complete these sentences.

1. The bird sat on its ___ ___ ___ ___ ___ in the cage.
2. I got a star when I came ___ ___ ___ ___ ___ in the race.
3. A nurse tied up my arm when it was ___ ___ ___ ___.
4. The girl put her new ___ ___ ___ ___ ___ in her bag.
5. At school, we ___ ___ ___ ___ ___ to read and spell.

  ISBN: 9781925726367

r controlled vowel sound  as in *corn*

Use this QR code to watch and listen to the **letter OR** sound cards below

There are different ways to spell the **or** sound as in corn.
These words also have the **or** sound.
Look at the pictures. Read the words. See the part that spells the **or** sound.

ball

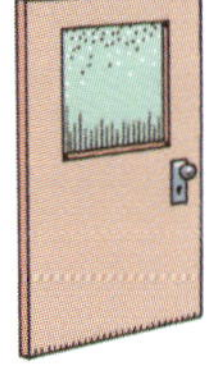

door

hawk

sauce

thought

  ISBN: 9781925726367

r controlled vowel sound or as in *corn*

Each of these words has the 'or' sound as in 'corn'. Read the words. Underline or highlight the letters that spell the 'or' sound.

or	fork	sport	storm	short
shorts	cork	port	north	torch
cord	corn	born	horn	form
more	sore	for	fore	four
store	force	score	snore	horse
shore	core	chores		
taught	caught	saw	paw	hawk
ball	fall	small	door	floor
talk	walk	sauce	your	board
war	bought	thought	fought	sure

Read the words. Draw lines to match them to the pictures.

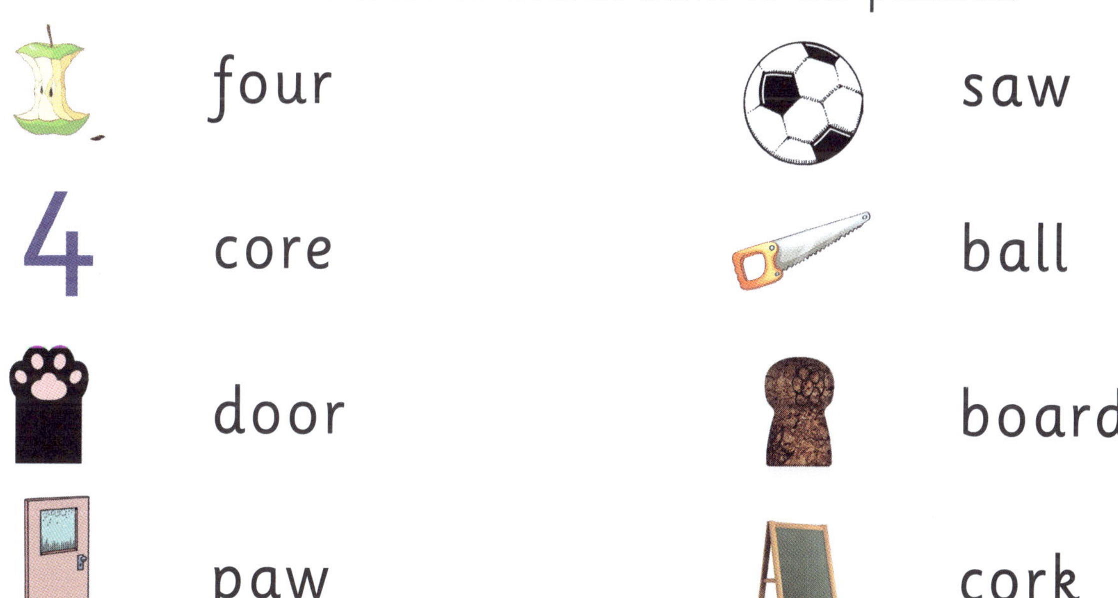

Choose a word with the **or** sound from the boxes above to complete these sentences.

1. The boys and girls like to play with a ____ ____ ____ ____ after school.
2. I hit my foot on a rock and made it ____ ____ ____ ____.
3. My mum ____ ____ ____ ____ ____ ____ me to ride a bike.
4. We went for a ____ ____ ____ ____ in the park.
5. I thought the book was mine but it is ____ ____ ____ ____ book.

  ISBN: 9781925726367

★ Unit 1 Review ★

'r' controlled vowel sounds 'ar', 'er' and 'or'

Read the words. Draw lines to match them to the pictures.

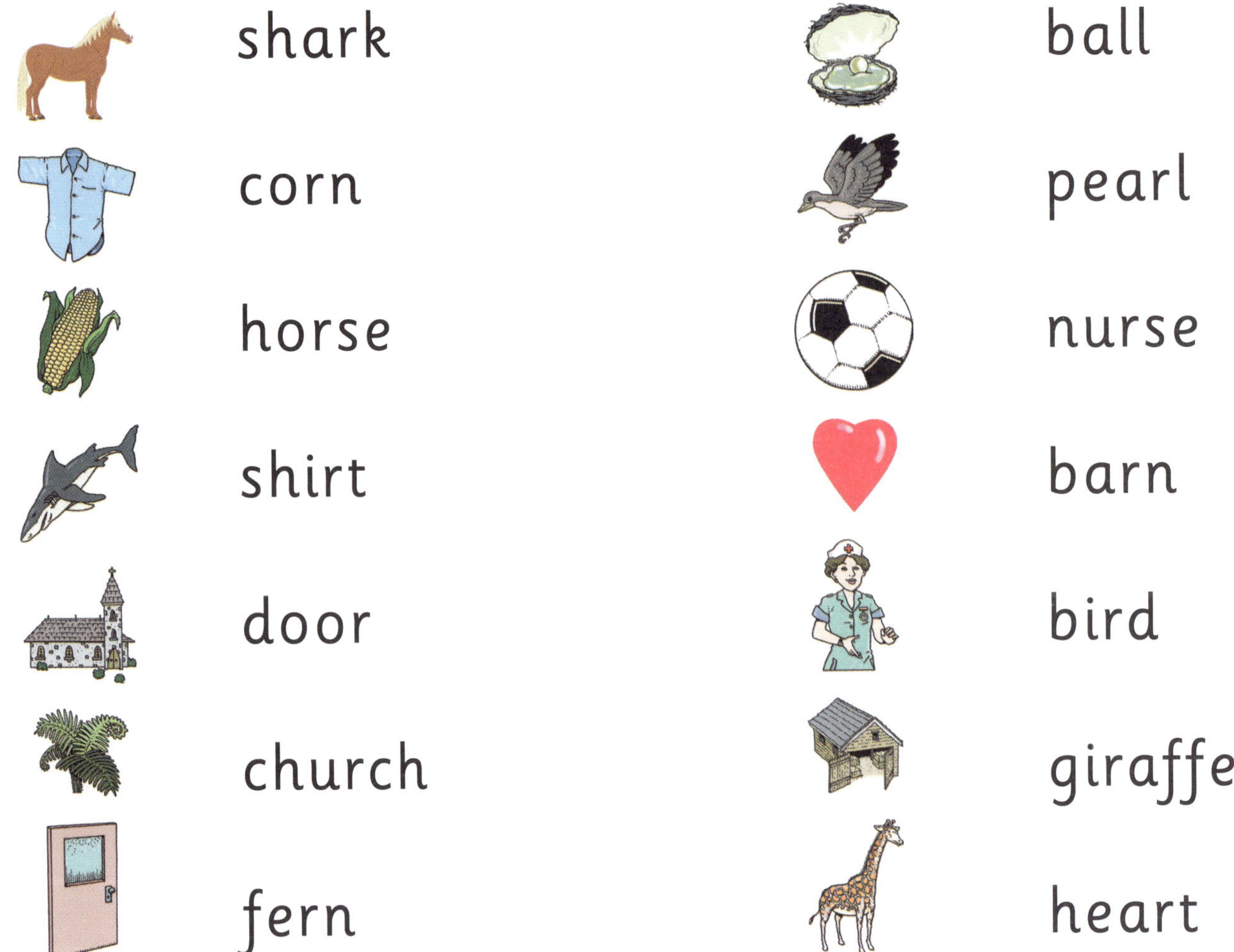

Say the names of the pictures below. Write the letters that are missing from each word.

c___ ___	sh___ ___ts	n___ ___se	f___ ___n
c___ ___n	f___ ___m	b___ ___d	ch___ ___ch

  ISBN: 9781925726367

'r' controlled vowel sounds 'ar', 'er' and 'or'

Read and draw.

Write letters to complete each word.
Then draw a picture of the word you made.

st__ __	b__ __n	f__ __n
sk__ __t	h__ __se	p__ __se

Choose the correct word

Look at the pictures. Read the pairs of words. Circle the correct word.

shirt shert	jer jar	shurk shark
fern firn	borl ball	curl cerl
berd bird	barn born	4 four for

  ISBN: 9781925726367

High frequency words – Unit 1

Here are some high frequency words to learn by sight.

giraffe	half	heart	laugh	were
one	old	two	under	grass

Reading and Comprehension

Read the story.

The Hurt Bird

One day, an old woman was in her yard. She dug in the dirt. She had some ferns to plant. The old woman had a cat with black fur. Her cat lay in the grass under the fir tree near the back door.

A bird flew down to the grass. The cat saw the bird. The old woman saw it too. Its wing was hurt. It had a sharp beak but that did not stop the old woman. The old woman put the bird in her scarf. She drove it to the vet in her car. It was not far.

The vet nurse took the bird from the old woman. She held it in her arms. "The vet will fix the bird," said the nurse. "The bird will fly soon." The old woman took out her purse. "No," said the nurse. "You do not need to pay. You have a good heart."

Write or tick the correct answer.

1. Where did the old woman see the bird?
   - ☐ a. In the tree
   - ☐ b. On the grass
   - ☐ c. In her car
   - ☐ d. At the vet's
2. Where did the old woman take the bird?
   - ☐ a. To the tree
   - ☐ b. To the back yard
   - ☐ c. To her house
   - ☐ d. To the vet
3. Why did the old woman take the bird to the vet?
   - ☐ a. It had a sharp beak.
   - ☐ b. Its wing was hurt.
   - ☐ c. It was not far.
   - ☐ d. She did not have to pay.
4. Why did the old woman dig in the dirt?
   - ☐ a. To plant some ferns
   - ☐ b. To hide the cat
   - ☐ c. To see the bird
   - ☐ d. To plant a tree
5. The cat's fur was ____________.
6. What did the old woman put the bird in?
   - ☐ a. A box
   - ☐ b. A scarf
   - ☐ c. Her pet cat
   - ☐ d. Her purse
7. What part of the bird was hurt?
   - ☐ a. Its wing
   - ☐ b. Its beak
   - ☐ c. Its foot
   - ☐ d. Its tail
8. Was the cat hurt?
   - ☐ a. Yes
   - ☐ b. No
9. Who will fix the bird?
   - ☐ a. The old woman
   - ☐ b. The cat
   - ☐ c. The nurse
   - ☐ d. The vet
10. When will the bird fly?
    - ☐ a. In one day
    - ☐ b. In two days
    - ☐ c. In six days
    - ☐ d. Soon

Choose words from the box to complete each sentence.

shirt	laugh	farm	horse	giraffe
barn	dirt	corn	stir	bird

1. When I went to the zoo, I saw a ___ ___ ___ ___ ___ ___ ___.
2. When my Dad tells a joke, he makes me ___ ___ ___ ___ ___.
3. The girl rode her ___ ___ ___ ___ ___ to school.
4. I saw a ___ ___ ___ ___ fly high in the sky.
5. Sheep and goats sleep in a ___ ___ ___ ___ on a ___ ___ ___ ___.
6. My big brother likes to eat ___ ___ ___ ___ on the cob.
7. Tim put on a clean ___ ___ ___ ___ ___ to go out for lunch.
8. If you spray water on the ___ ___ ___ ___, it will be mud.
9. I like to help Mum ___ ___ ___ ___ the mix when she makes a cake.

  ISBN: 9781925726367

Vowel digraph  as in *cow*

You already know that the letters 'ow' can be used to spell the long vowel sound 'o' as in bow and show. Now you will learn that they can be used to spell the 'ow' sound as in cow and crown.

Use this QR code to watch and listen to the **letter OW** sound cards below

 cow	 crown
 house	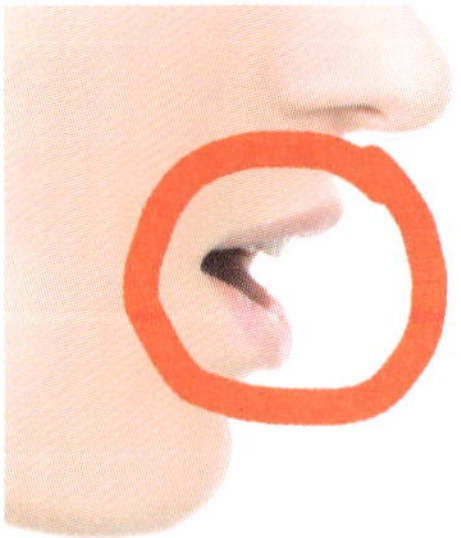 mouth

There are different ways to spell the **ow** sound as in cow.
These words also have the **ow** sound.
Look at the pictures. Read the words. See the part that spells the **ow** sound.

 clown

 cloud

 pouch

 bough

 plough

Vowel digraph ow as in *cow*

Each of these words has the 'ow' sound as in 'cow'. Read the words. Underline or highlight the letters that spell the 'ow' sound.

ow	cow	bow	brow	brown
frown	crown	down	clown	growl
gown	how	howl	now	prowl
town	owl	crowd		
out	house	loud	mouth	cloud
count	flour	proud	sound	bounce
sprout	shout	round	found	wound
mouse	trout	scout	pouch	south
plough	bough	drought		

Read the words. Draw lines to match them to the pictures.

Choose a word with the **ow** sound from the boxes above to complete these sentences.

1. The little grey ___ ___ ___ ___ ___ ran up the clock.
2. A big ___ ___ ___ ___ ___ met at the town hall.
3. Mum could not bake a cake as she had no ___ ___ ___ ___ ___.
4. When the king lost his ___ ___ ___ ___ ___, he was sad.
5. When it rains a lot, the ___ ___ ___ ___ ___ ___ ___ will break.
6. The boy made no ___ ___ ___ ___ ___ when he came to the door.

  ISBN: 9781925726367

Vowel digraph  oi as in *coin*

Use this QR code to watch and listen to the **letter OI** sound cards below

coin

soil

boy

toy

There are different ways to spell the **oi** sound as in coin. These words also have the **oi** sound.
Look at the pictures. Read the words. See the part that spells the **oi** sound.

oil

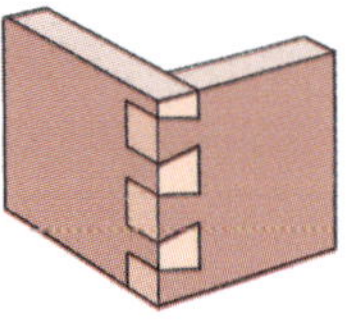

joint

coil

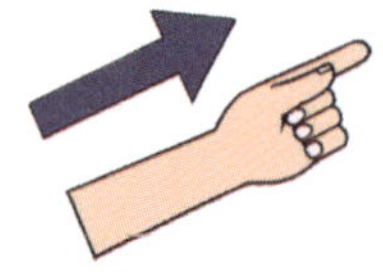

point

buoy

  ISBN: 9781925726367

Vowel digraph oi as in *coin*

Each of these words has the 'oi' sound as in 'coin'. Read the words. Underline or highlight the letters that spell the 'oi' sound.

oi	noise	coin	join	soil
oil	boil	void	coil	spoil
moist	joint	groin	voice	hoist
point	choice	oink	foil	toil
toy	ploy	joy	soy	coy
boy	buoy			

Read the words. Draw lines to match them to the pictures.

Choose a word with the **oi** sound from the boxes above to complete these sentences.

1. I heard a loud ___ ___ ___ ___ ___ in the barn.
2. Dad put my lunch in ___ ___ ___ ___ to keep it fresh.
3. When the water starts to ___ ___ ___ ___ , it is very hot.
4. The little girl has a new ___ ___ ___ truck.
5. If you leave milk in the sun, it will ___ ___ ___ ___ ___.
6. I had no ___ ___ ___ ___ ___ ___ but to run away.
7. The man dug the ___ ___ ___ ___ to plant some seeds.
8. The snake was wound round in a ___ ___ ___ ___.

  ISBN: 9781925726367

Vowel trigraph 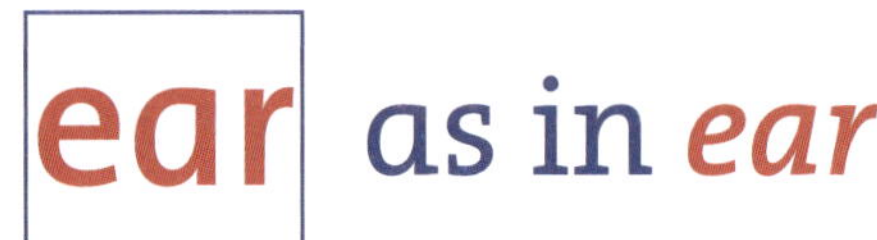 as in *ear*

ear

Use this QR code to watch and listen to the **letter EAR** sound cards below

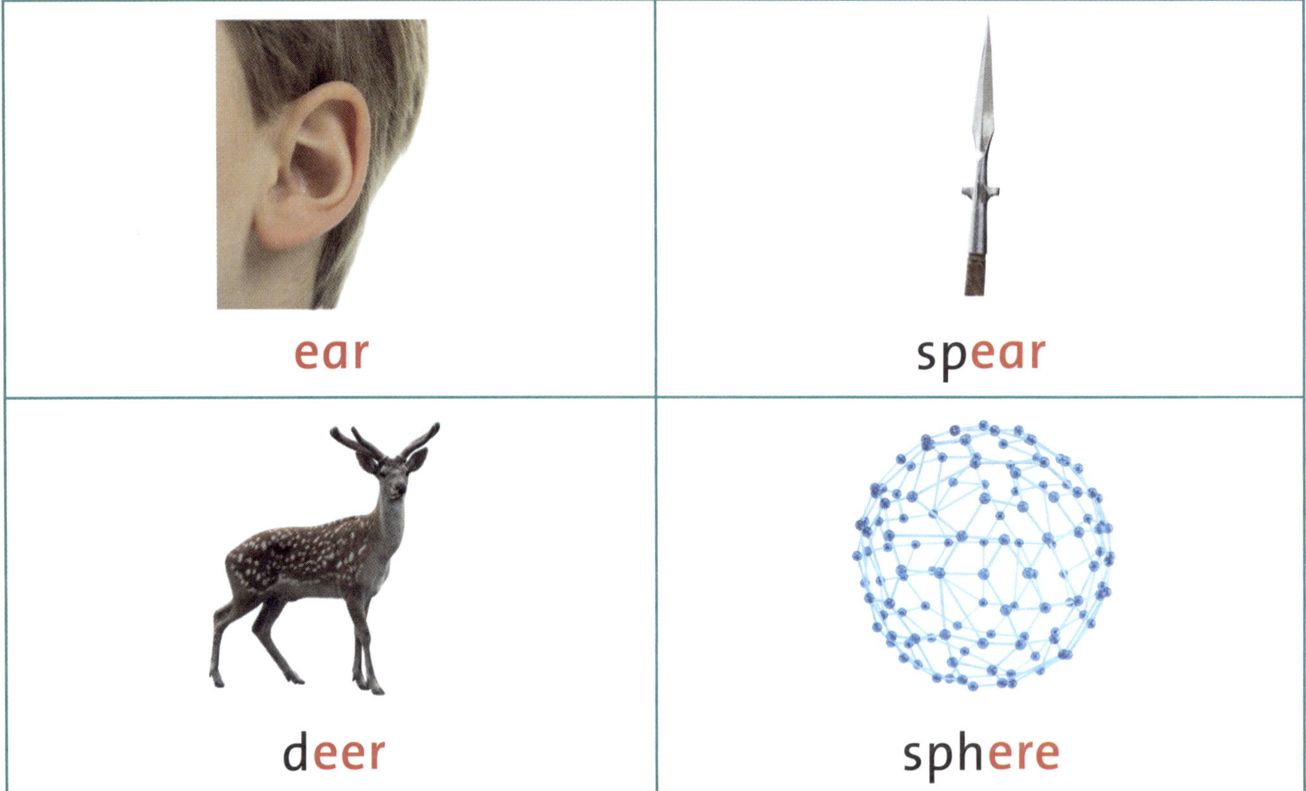

There are different ways to spell the **ear** sound as in ear.
These words also have the **ear** sound.
Look at the pictures. Read the words. See the part that spells the **ear** sound.

beard	pier	sphere	steer	tear

  ISBN: 9781925726367

Vowel trigraph ear as in *ear*

Each of these words has the 'ear' sound as in 'ear'. Read the words. Underline or highlight the letters that spell the 'ear' sound.

ear	fear	rear	hear	dear
near	gear	sear	tear	spear
clear	year	beard		
beer	deer	steer	cheer	veer
sheer	peer	sneer		
pier	fierce	weir	sphere	here

Read the words. Draw lines to match them to the pictures.

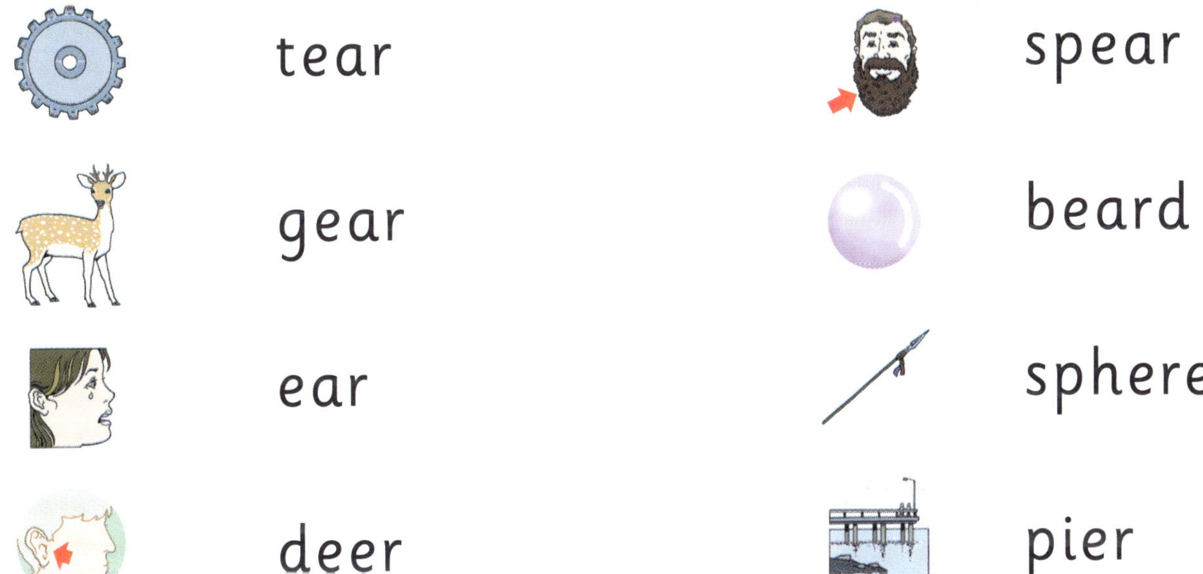

Choose a word with the **ear** sound from the boxes above to complete these sentences.

1. The man at the shop had a long ____ ____ ____ ____ ____.
2. We had to wait all ____ ____ ____ ____ to get a new car.
3. A ____ ____ ____ ____ ____ went up from the crowd when their team came first.
4. I like to fish from the ____ ____ ____ ____ with my dad.
5. The Earth is in the shape of a ____ ____ ____ ____ ____ ____.
6. Kate left her book at school ____ ____ ____ ____ the gate.
7. We saw a small herd of ____ ____ ____ ____ at the zoo.
8. The boy shed a ____ ____ ____ ____ when he was sad.

  ISBN: 9781925726367

Vowel trigraph  air as in *hair*

Use this QR code to watch and listen to the **letter AIR** sound cards below

 hair	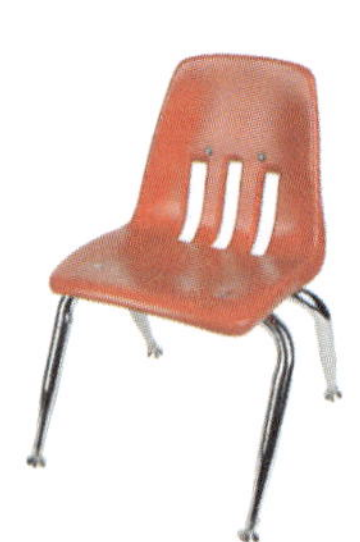 chair
 bear	 hare

There are different ways to spell the **air** sound as in hair.
These words also have the **air** sound.
Look at the pictures. Read the words. See the part that spells the **air** sound.

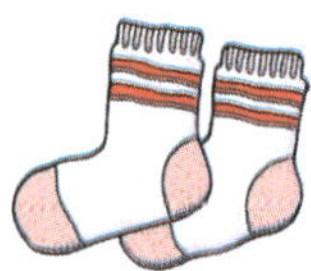	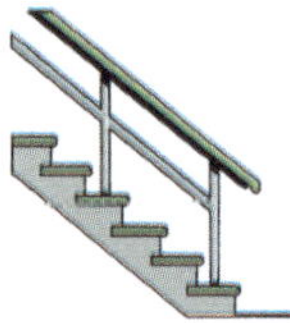	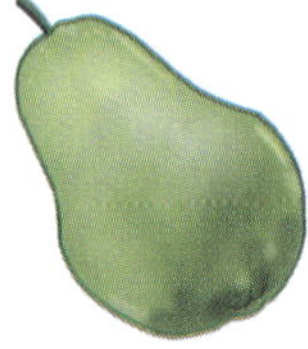		
pair	stairs	pear	square	mayor

  ISBN: 9781925726367

Vowel trigraph air as in *hair*

Each of these words has the 'air' sound as in 'hair'. Read the words. Underline or highlight the letters that spell the 'air' sound.

air	fair	lair	hair	pair
chair	stairs	flair		
bear	tear	pear	wear	
care	fare	share	mare	dare
bare	rare	hare	scare	spare
glare	square	flare	snare	stare
where	there	their	mayor	prayer

Read the words. Draw lines to match them to the pictures.

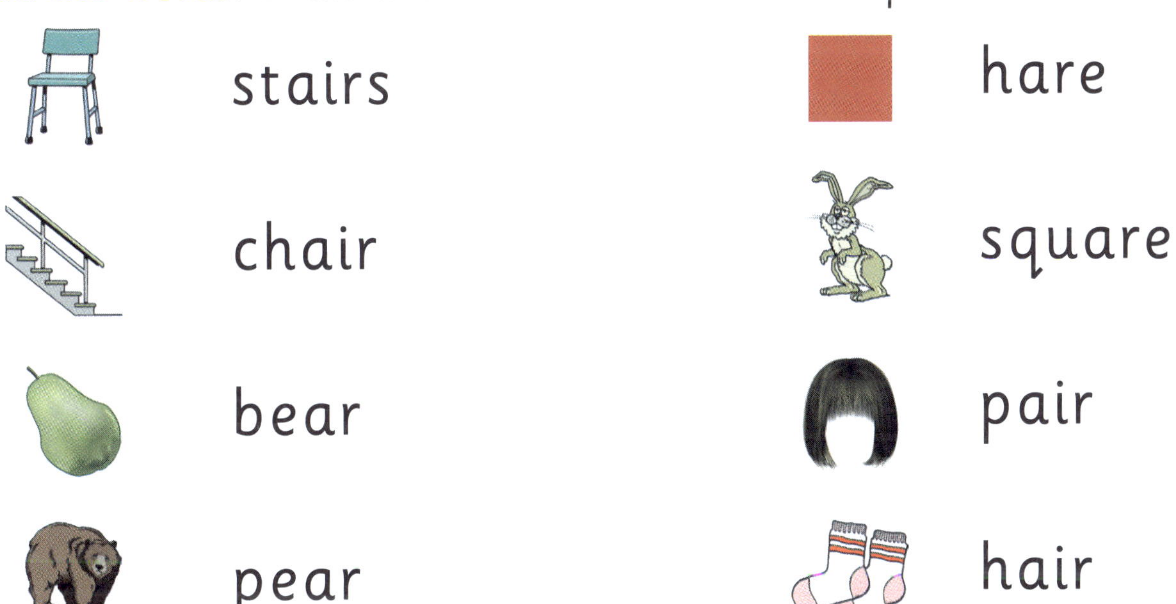

Choose a word with the **air** sound from the boxes above to complete these sentences.

1. Mum said the twins had to ___ ___ ___ ___ ___ the toys.
2. My brother tries to ___ ___ ___ ___ ___ me at night.
3. I had a ___ ___ ___ ___ in my lunch.
4. A little brown hare was caught in a ___ ___ ___ ___ ___.
5. My sister likes it when I brush her ___ ___ ___ ___.
6. Dad gave me some coins to pay my bus ___ ___ ___ ___.
7. A crowd met at the town hall to see the ___ ___ ___ ___ ___.
8. The boys and girls took ___ ___ ___ ___ ___ books home.

  ISBN: 9781925726367

★ Unit 2 Review ★

Vowel digraphs 'ow' and 'oi' and vowel trigraphs 'ear' and 'air'

Read the words. Draw lines to match them to the pictures.

Say the names of the pictures below. Write the letters that are missing from each word.

  ISBN: 9781925726367

Vowel digraphs 'ow' and 'oi' and vowel trigraphs 'ear' and 'air' Read and draw.

Write letters to complete each word.
Then draw a picture of the word you made.

h___ ___se	c___ ___	p___ ___nt
b___ ___ ___	b___ ___	p___ ___ ___

Choose the correct word

Look at the pictures. Read the pairs of words. Circle the correct word.

  ISBN: 9781925726367

High frequency words – Unit 2

Here are some high frequency words to learn by sight.

children	people	happy	of	onto

Reading and Comprehension

Read the story.

The Circus

One day the fair came to our town. The people set up the fair in the show grounds. There were a lot of vans and one big tent. That night, Tim and Sam went to the fair. They sat on chairs near the ring with all the children. Sam held her toy bear tight. First, a clown came out into the ring. The clown did tricks. Each time he did a trick, the crowd would cheer. Sam put her hands on her ears. Her bear fell to the ground.

"That noise is too loud," she said with a frown.

"Did the noise scare you?" said Tim.

"No," said Sam, but there was a tear in her eye and her mouth was down.

A man with a beard and a kind voice gave Sam her bear.

"Here you are," he said.

Sam gave the man a shy smile. She was happy now.

When the show came to an end, the crowd gave a big cheer. The clown took a bow.

Write or tick the correct answer.

1. Where was the fair set up?
   - ☐ a. In the tent
   - ☐ b. Near the town
   - ☐ c. In the show grounds
   - ☐ d. At our house
2. When did Tim and Sam go to the fair?
   - ☐ a. After school
   - ☐ b. At night
   - ☐ c. In the day
   - ☐ d. Last week
3. Where did Tim and Sam sit?
   - ☐ a. With their mum and dad
   - ☐ b. Near the ring
   - ☐ c. At the back of the tent
   - ☐ d. In the ring
4. What did the clown do?
   - ☐ a. Made Sam cry
   - ☐ b. Tricks
   - ☐ c. Rode a bike
   - ☐ d. Gave Sam her toy bear
5. A lot of people is a ______________.
6. Why did Sam put her hands on her ears?
   - ☐ a. The clown gave her a fright.
   - ☐ b. Her toy bear fell on the ground.
   - ☐ c. The cheer was too loud.
   - ☐ d. Her ears were sore.
7. How did Sam feel when the noise was loud?
   - ☐ a. Happy
   - ☐ b. Sad
   - ☐ c. Proud
   - ☐ d. Full of joy
8. Who gave Sam her bear when it fell?
   - ☐ a. A man with a beard
   - ☐ b. Tim
   - ☐ c. The clown
9. What did the crowd do when the show came to an end?
   - ☐ a. Stood up
   - ☐ b. Went home
   - ☐ c. Gave a big cheer.
   - ☐ d. Left the tent
10. How did Sam feel at the end of the show?______________

Choose words from the box to complete each sentence.

steer	wear	howl	year	flour
pair	buoys	pear	boil	share

1. The dogs would ___ ___ ___ ___ when the moon was full.
2. I put one cup of ___ ___ ___ ___ ___ in the bowl to make a cake.
3. You have to ___ ___ ___ ___ the water to cook an egg.
4. The ___ ___ ___ ___ ___ tell the ships which way to go.
5. I will join the school chess team this ___ ___ ___ ___.
6. I can ___ ___ ___ ___ ___ my bike to go past the rocks.
7. Tan put on a clean ___ ___ ___ ___ of shorts to go out for lunch.
8. Bree cut her ___ ___ ___ ___ in two to ___ ___ ___ ___ ___ with her sister.
9. I like to ___ ___ ___ ___ my best shirt when we go out.

  ISBN: 9781925726367

Consonant trigraphs tch as in *match* and dge as in *bridge*

You already know some consonant digraphs in which 2 letters are used to represent one phoneme, for example: sh, ch, th, ph, wh. Now you will learn some trigraphs in which 3 letters are used to represent one phoneme. The trigraph 'tch' represents the same sound as 'ch'. The trigraph 'dge' represents the same sound as soft 'g' or 'j'.

Use this QR code to watch and listen to the **letter TCH/DGE** sound cards below

tch/dge

 match	 witch
 bridge	fridge

Look at the pictures. Say the words.

Colour the words that have the **tch** sound green. Colour the words that have the **dge** words yellow.

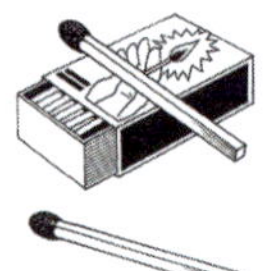  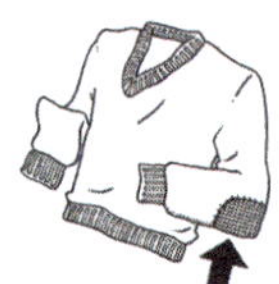 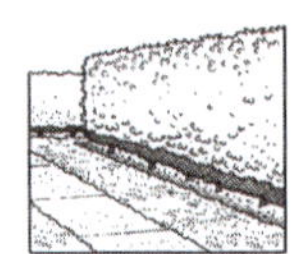   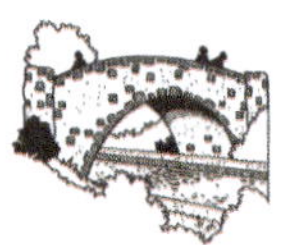

  ISBN: 9781925726367

Consonant trigraphs tch as in *match* and dge as in *bridge*

Each of these words has the 'ch' sound as in 'match'. Read the words. Underline or highlight the letters that spell the 'tch' sound.

tch	catch	hatch	patch	batch
match	fetch	sketch	itch	witch
snitch	ditch	pitch	stitch	watch
hutch				

Each of these words has the 'j' sound as in 'bridge'. Read the words. Underline or highlight the letters that spell the 'dge' sound.

dge	badge	edge	hedge	ridge
bridge	fridge	lodge	smudge	fudge
nudge	judge			

Read the words. Draw lines to match them to the pictures.

 match  fudge

 patch  judge

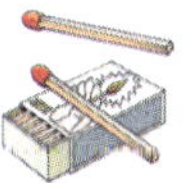 witch  bridge

 badge  fridge

 hedge  watch

'ch' or 'tch'?
'tch' is never used at the beginning of a word. At the end of a word, 'tch' usually follows a short vowel sound.

'g' or 'dge'?
'g' is usually used to spell the soft 'g' sound when it follows a long vowel as in stage and cage or an 'n' as in orange and change. We usually use 'dge' after a short vowel sound as in bridge and fudge.

Choose a word with the **tch** or **dge** sound from the boxes above to complete these sentences.

1. The boy threw the ball too high for me to _____ _____ _____ _____ _____.
2. We must not go near the _____ _____ _____ _____ of the cliff.
3. The paint was still wet and I put a _____ _____ _____ _____ _____ _____ on it.
4. The boy got a _____ _____ _____ _____ _____ _____ in his side when he ran fast.
5. The truck went too fast and went into a _____ _____ _____ _____ _____.
6. We put milk in the _____ _____ _____ _____ _____ _____ to keep it cool.

  ISBN: 9781925726367

Three-letter consonant blends  

In digraphs and trigraphs, the letters represent just one sound. In a blend, each of the letters represents its own sound. Each letter is sounded separately and then blended.

scr/str

Use this QR code to watch and listen to the **letter SCR/STR** sound cards below

 s-c-r-een	 s-c-r-ew
 s-t-r-ipes	 s-t-r-eet

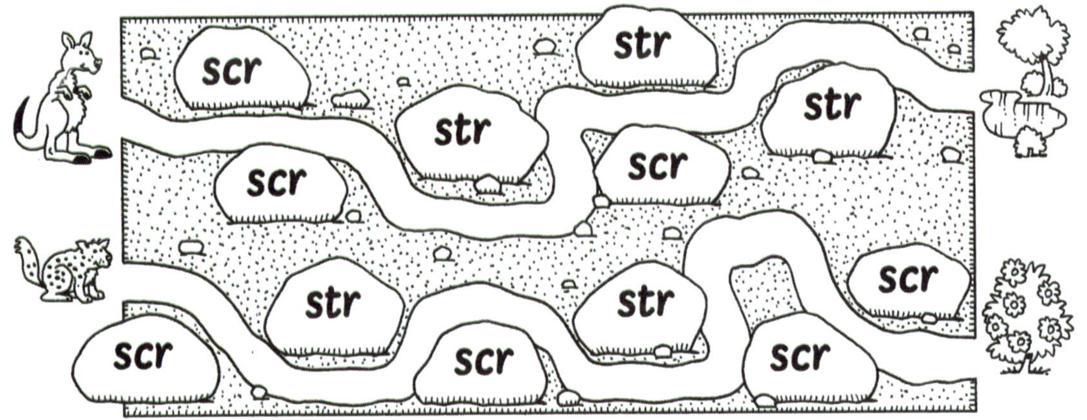

Look at the letters on the rocks. Colour the rocks with **scr** green, and the rocks with **str** blue. Practise sounding each letter then blending them as you go.

  ISBN: 9781925726367

Three-letter consonant blends scr, str

Each of these words begins with the 3-letter blend 'scr' as in 'scratch'. Read the words. Underline or highlight the letters that spell the 'scr' blend.

Remember to sound each letter in the blend separately.

scr	screen	script	scream	scribe
scrap	screw	scrub	screech	scram
scrape	scratch			

Each of these words begins with the 3-letter blend 'str' as in 'stripes'. Read the words. Underline or highlight the letters that spell the 'str' blend.

str	stripes	strain	strong	strap
strand	stray	strip	street	stretch
strange	straight	strict	string	stress
struck	stream	strength	strike	straw

Read the words. Draw lines to match them to the pictures.

 scratch

 screw

 street

 stripes

 scraps

 straw

 screen

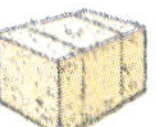 stream

Choose a word with the **scr** or **str** sound from the boxes above to complete these sentences.

1. I have to ____ ____ ____ ____ ____ my legs after I play in the dirt.
2. Dad told us to go ____ ____ ____ ____ ____ ____ ____ ____ home after school.
3. I had to use all my ____ ____ ____ ____ ____ ____ ____ ____ to pick up the big box.
4. Mum lets me ____ ____ ____ ____ ____ ____ the bowl when she cooks cakes.
5. A ____ ____ ____ ____ ____ cat comes to our house each day.
6. One of the boys was ____ ____ ____ ____ ____ ____ by a ball at play time.
7. We put all our ____ ____ ____ ____ ____ ____ in the bin after lunch.

  ISBN: 9781925726367

Three-letter consonant blends  

These are blends. Remember, in a blend, each of the letters represents its own sound. Each letter is sounded separately and then blended.

spr/spl

Use this QR code to watch and listen to the **letter SPR/SPL** sound cards below

 s-p-r-ing	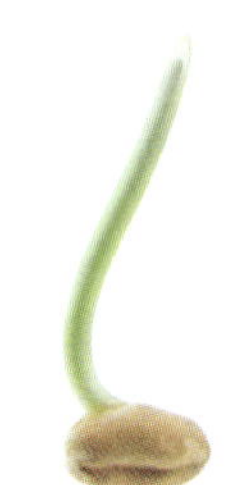 s-p-r-out
 s-p-l-ash	 s-p-l-its

Look at the letters on the rocks. Colour the rocks with **spr** blue, and the rocks with **spl** pink. Practise sounding each letter then blending them as you go.

  ISBN: 9781925726367

Three-letter consonant blends spr, spl

Each of these words begins with the 3-letter blend 'spr' as in 'spring'. Read the words. Underline or highlight the letters that spell the 'spr' blend.

Remember to sound each letter in the blend separately.

spr	spray	spree	sprig	spread
spring	sprain	sprout	sprite	sprawl
sprint	spruce	spry		

Each of these words begins with the 3-letter blend 'spl' as in 'splash'. Read the words. Underline or highlight the letters that spell the 'spl' blend.

spl	splash	splat	splay	split
splosh	spleen	splint	splice	

Read the words. Draw lines to match them to the pictures.

 spray

 spring

 sprout

 splash

 splits

 splint

Choose a word with the **spr** or **spl** sound from the boxes above to complete these sentences.

1. I like to ___ ___ ___ ___ ___ ___ jam on my warm bread.
2. The fish made a big ___ ___ ___ ___ ___ ___ in the water.
3. The boy had his arm in a ___ ___ ___ ___ ___ ___ after he hurt it.
4. I can run fast and win in a ___ ___ ___ ___ ___ ___ race.
5. The cat went ___ ___ ___ ___ ___ on the wet mat.
6. I like it when the days warm up in ___ ___ ___ ___ ___ ___.
7. We water our seeds and watch for them to ___ ___ ___ ___ ___ ___.
8. The children have fun in the ___ ___ ___ ___ ___ from the hose.

  ISBN: 9781925726367

Digraph blends 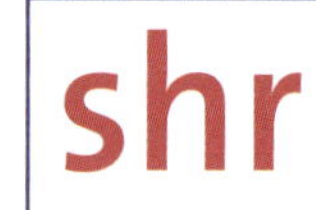 

You already know the digraphs 'sh' as in 'shop' and 'th' as in 'that'. When a consonant digraph blends with another consonant, it is called a digraph blend.

shr/thr

Use this QR code to watch and listen to the **letter SHR/THR** sound cards below

 sh-r-imp	 sh-r-ub
 th-r-ee	 th-r-one

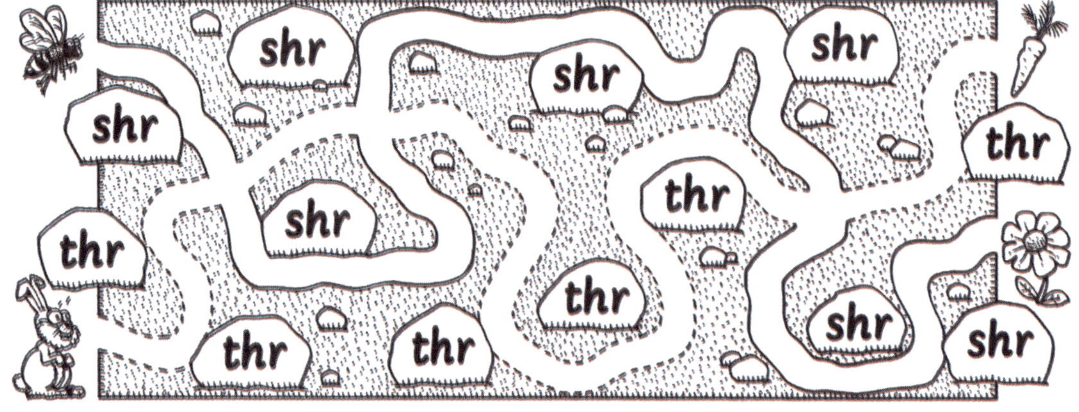

Look at the letters on the rocks. Colour the path with **shr** orange. Colour the path with **thr** green. Practise sounding the digraph and the letter then blending them as you go.

  ISBN: 9781925726367

Digraph blends shr, thr

Each of these words begins with the digraph blend 'shr' as in 'shrimp'. Read the words. Underline or highlight the letters that spell the 'shr' digraph blend.

Remember to sound the digraph and then the consonant.

shr	shrimp	shrine	shred	shrub
shrug	shrank	shrunk	shrink	shrewd
shrill	shrike	shroud	shriek	

Each of these words begins with the digraph blend 'thr' as in 'three'. Read the words. Underline or highlight the letters that spell the 'thr' blend.

thr	three	throw	threw	thread
throb	throat	thrust	thrill	throng
throne	thrush	through		

Read the words. Draw lines to match them to the pictures.

 shrub

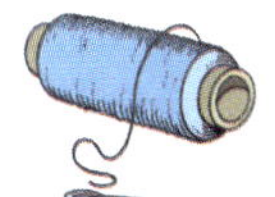 throne

 shrug

 thread

Choose a word with the **shr** or **thr** sound from the boxes above to complete these sentences.

1. My shirt was too small after it __ __ __ __ __ __ in the wash.
2. The big boy __ __ __ __ __ the ball that broke the glass.
3. It is a __ __ __ __ __ __ when we go on rides at the show.
4. When we play hide and seek, I hide near a __ __ __ __ __.
5. My little brother can count: one, two, __ __ __ __ __.
6. I put my hands on my ears when I heard a __ __ __ __ __ __ sound.
7. The king sat on his __ __ __ __ __ __ and told the people what to do.
8. When the girl's __ __ __ __ __ __ was sore, she could not talk.

  ISBN: 9781925726367

⋆ Unit 3 Review ⋆

Consonant trigraphs, 3-letter consonant blends and digraph blends: tch, dge, scr, str, spr, spl, shr, thr

Read the words. Draw lines to match them to the pictures.

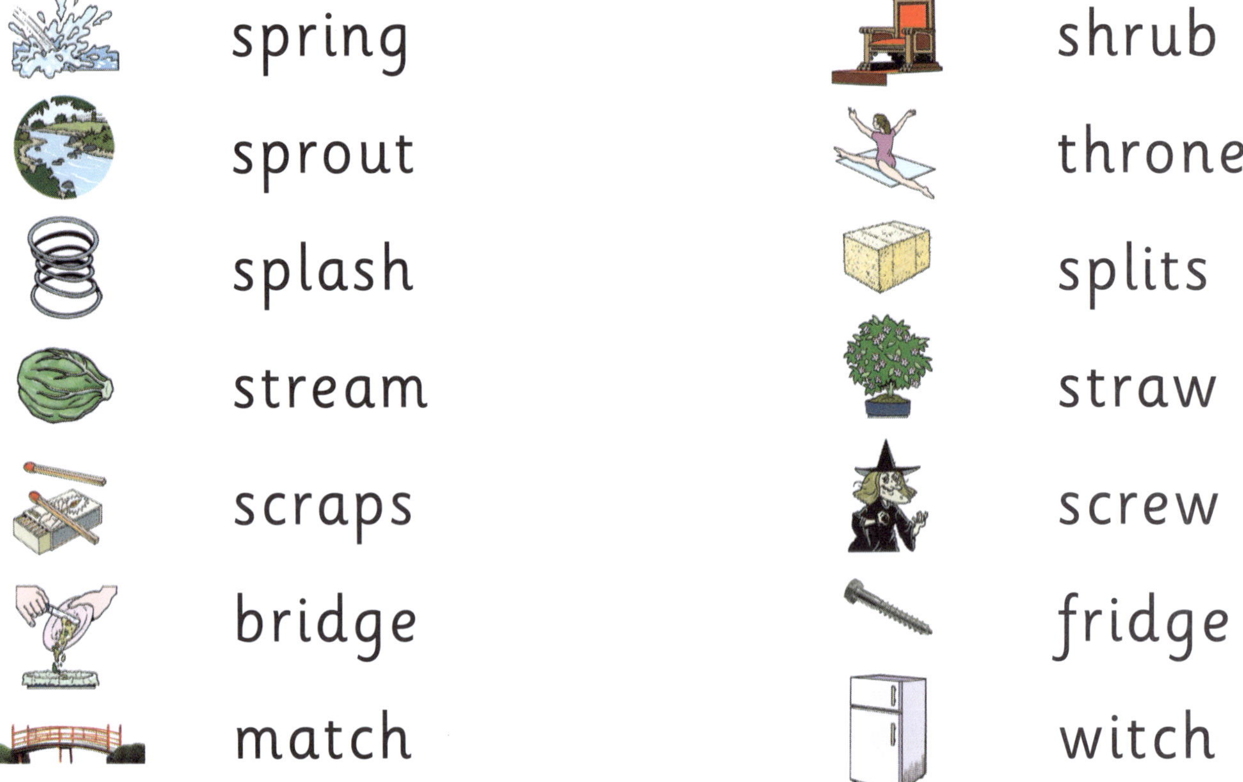

Say the names of the pictures below. Write the letters that are missing from each word.

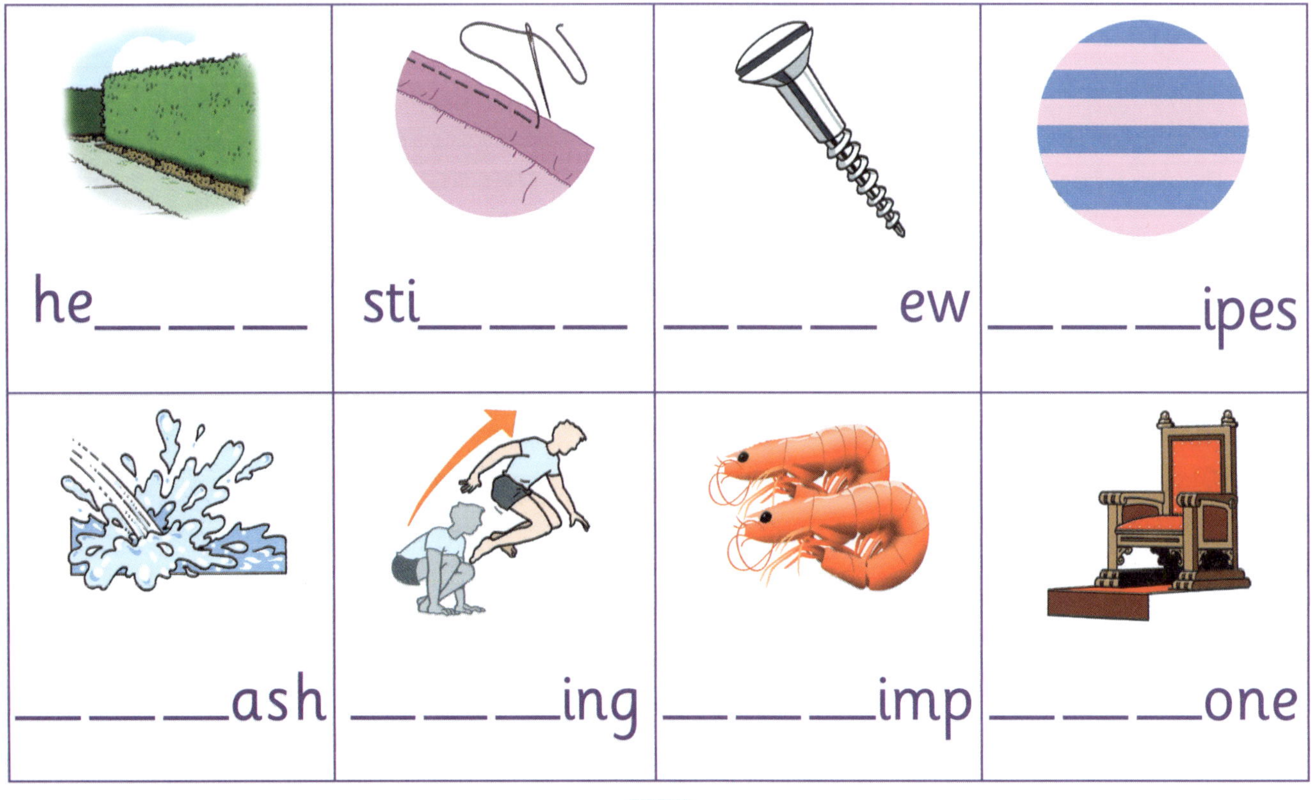

  ISBN: 9781925726367

Consonant trigraphs, 3-letter consonant blends and digraph blends: tch, dge, scr, str, spr, spl, shr, thr

Read and draw.

Write letters to complete each word.
Then draw a picture of the word you made.

__ __ __ ee	bri __ __ __	__ __ __ eam
wi __ __ __	__ __ __ ub	__ __ __ one

Choose the correct word

Look at the pictures. Read the pairs of words. Circle the correct word.

bridge brige	shrink splint	mach match
shrub scrub	tree three	splay spray
spits splits	stream scream	screw scroo

  ISBN: 9781925726367

High Frequency Words — Unit 3

Here are some high frequency words to learn by sight.

so	over	asked	didn't	suddenly
morning	very	only	across	many

Reading and Comprehension

Read the story.

Fish for Lunch

One morning in spring, three children went for a ride on their bikes. They rode straight down the street, through the scrub, across the bridge and down to the stream. They left their bikes near a small shrub. Then they sat on the bank at the edge of the stream under the bridge.

Jade threw her line into the water. "I hope we catch some fish," she said.

"Did you hear that strange noise?" said Blake.

"What noise?" asked Reece.

"It went scratch, scratch, scratch over the bridge," said Blake.

Suddenly, there was a big splash. The children got wet from the spray. It gave them a fright, but they didn't scream.

"Who is there?" said Reece.

"A mean witch," said a shrill voice.

"It's only Sage," said Blake. "She likes to scare us."

"Good try," said Reece.

Just then, Jade felt a tug on her line. "Watch this," she said.

Jade had to use all her strength to land the fish. It was so big, they all had fish for lunch.

  ISBN: 9781925726367

Write or tick the correct answer.

1. How did the children get to the stream?
   - ☐ a. In a bus
   - ☐ b. In a car
   - ☐ c. On their bikes
   - ☐ d. In a train
2. When did they go to the stream?
   - ☐ a. One night in spring
   - ☐ b. One day after lunch
   - ☐ c. After school
   - ☐ d. One morning in spring
3. Where did the children sit?
   - ☐ a. Near a shrub
   - ☐ b. Under the bridge
   - ☐ c. In the water
   - ☐ d. On the bridge
4. What did Blake hear?
   - ☐ a. A strange noise
   - ☐ b. A car go over the bridge
   - ☐ c. Reece scream
   - ☐ d. A loud bang
5. What gave the children a fright?
   - ☐ a. A mean witch
   - ☐ b. A big splash
   - ☐ c. A car horn
   - ☐ d. A loud voice
6. Who tried to give the children a fright?
   - ☐ a. Reece
   - ☐ b. Blake
   - ☐ c. Jade
   - ☐ d. Sage
7. What size was the fish Jade caught?
   - ☐ a. Big
   - ☐ b. Very big
   - ☐ c. Small
   - ☐ d. Very small
8. How many children were at the stream?
   - ☐ a. One
   - ☐ b. Two
   - ☐ c. Three
   - ☐ d. Four

Write the answers to these questions in sentences.

9. Where did the children put their bikes?

____

10. What do you think made the big splash in the water?

____

Choose words from the box to complete each sentence.

strong	fridge	spread	splash	hatch	through	scrub

1. When the eggs ___ ___ ___ ___ ___ we will have four little chicks.
2. We keep our milk and cheese in the ___ ___ ___ ___ ___ ___.
3. After we play in the mud, we have to ___ ___ ___ ___ ___ our legs.
4. I am so ___ ___ ___ ___ ___ ___ I can pick up a very big box.
5. I help my dad ___ ___ ___ ___ ___ ___ the soil when we lay the new turf.
6. We all like to ___ ___ ___ ___ ___ ___ in the water at the beach.
7. The children ran ___ ___ ___ ___ ___ ___ ___ the bush and down to the lake.

  ISBN: 9781925726367

Word families: verbs 1

s/ed/ing/er

Now you know how the letters are used to most often represent the sounds of the English language. You can use that knowledge to decode and spell most one-syllable words.
In this unit, you will learn to decode and spell words with more than one syllable where an ending is used to change the tense or form of verbs to create word families.

I play. You play.

We play.

They play.

He play**s**.

She play**s**.

We are play**ing**.

In the past (yesterday), we play**ed**.

We are play**ers**.

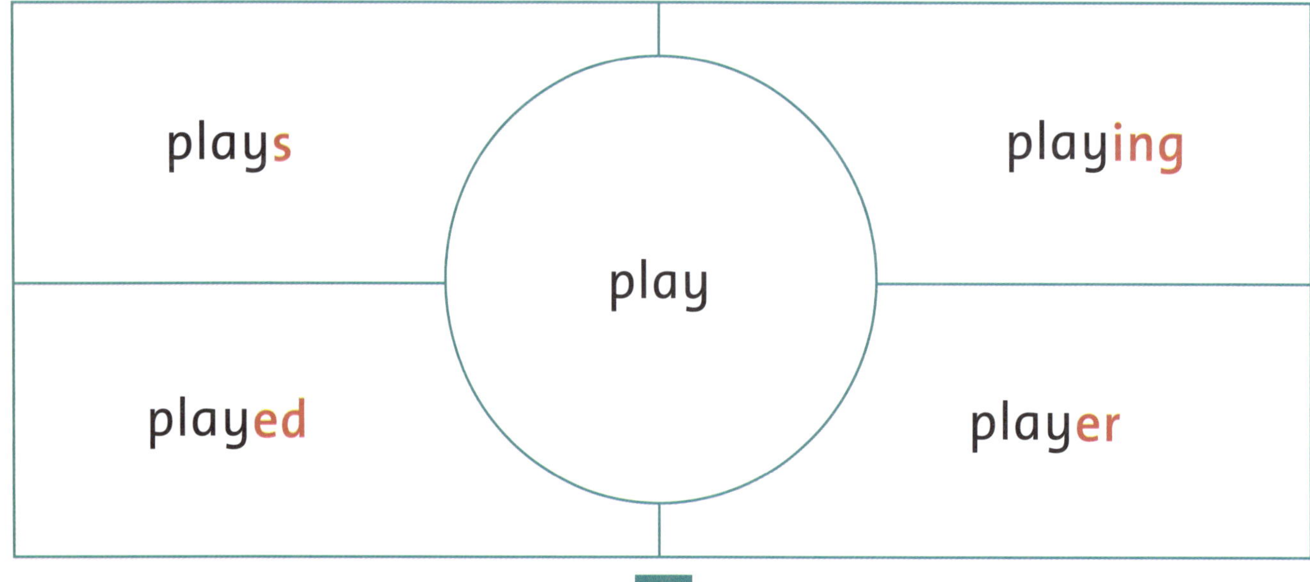

Word families: verbs — s/ed/ing/er

Read the words. Complete the table by adding the endings to the words. The first one is done for you. These verbs are *regular* verbs.

Verb	s	ing	ed	er
clean	cleans	cleaning	cleaned	cleaner
train				
bill				
stream				
walk				
jump				
count				
paint				
add				
blend				

Read the list of words ending with 'ed'. What do you notice?
When verbs end with a voiced consonant; for example, n, l and m, the letters 'ed' make the 'd' sound.
When the verbs end with an unvoiced consonant; for example, k, sh, p and x, the letters 'ed' make the 't' sound.
When the verbs end with a 't' or a 'd', the letters 'ed' make the 'ed' sound.

Some verbs are *irregular* verbs. Their past tense words do not follow the 'ed' pattern. Read the words. Complete the table. The past tense is completed for you.

Verb	s	ing	(past)	er
read			read	
draw			drew	
sweep			swept	
sing			sang	
tell			told	
blow			blew	

  ISBN: 9781925726367

Word families: verbs 2

s/ed/ing/er

Now you know about the endings that are used to change the tense or form of verbs. In this lesson, you will learn how the endings are added to verbs that end with the letter 'e'. When a verb ends with the letter 'e', we leave off the 'e' before adding the 'ing', 'ed' or 'er'.

I dance. You dance.

We dance.

They dance. He dances.

She dances.

We are dancing.

In the past (yesterday), we danced.

We are dancers.

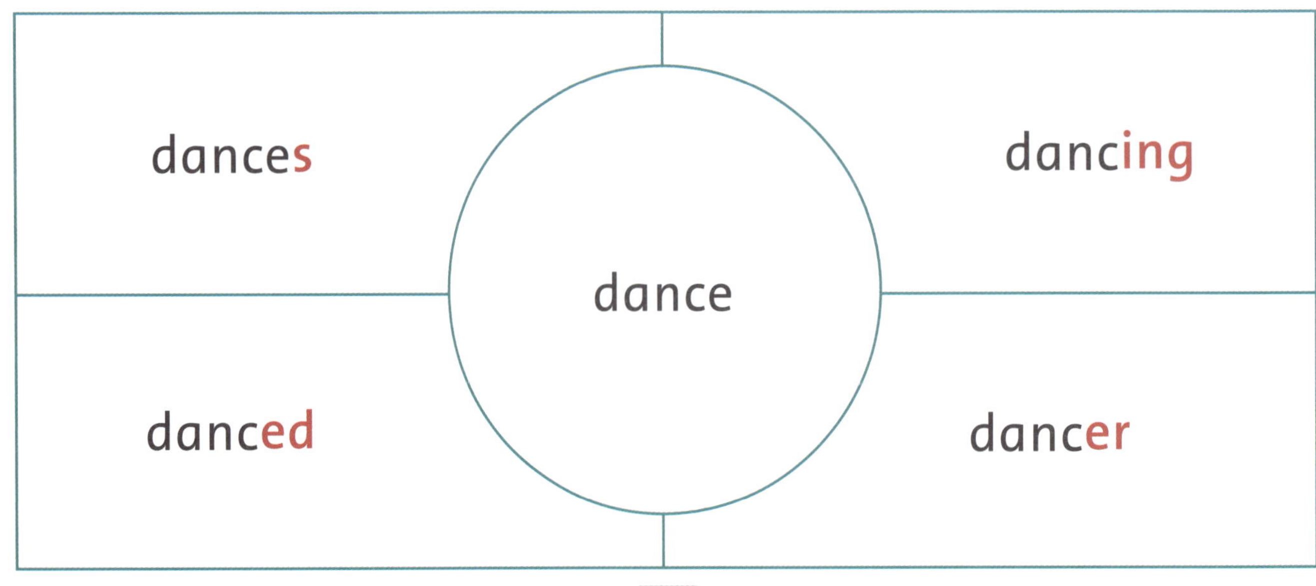

Word families: verbs — s/ed/ing/er

Read the words. Complete the table by adding the endings to the words. The first one is done for you. Remember to leave off the 'e' before adding 'ing', 'ed' or 'er'.
These verbs are *regular* verbs. Their past tense verbs end with 'ed'.

Verb	s	ing	ed	er
save	saves	saving	saved	saver
mine				
smile				
share				
bounce				
hope				
like				
joke				
hate				
taste				
shade				
grade				

Read the list of words ending with 'ed'. Did you remember?
When verbs end with a voiced consonant; for example, v, n, l and r, the letters 'ed' make the 'd' sound.
When the verbs end with an unvoiced consonant; for example, k, s and p, the letters 'ed' make the 't' sound.
When the verbs end with a 't' or a 'd', the letters 'ed' make the 'ed' sound.

Some verbs are *irregular* verbs. Their past tense words do not follow the 'ed' pattern.
Read the words. Complete the table. The past tense is completed for you.

Verb	s	ing	(past)	er
drive			drove	
ride			rode	
hide			hid	
rise			rose	
write			wrote	

  ISBN: 9781925726367

Word families: verbs 3

s/ed/ing/er

Now you know about the endings that are used to change the tense or form of verbs. In this lesson, you will learn how the endings are added to verbs that end with a short vowel and one consonant.

When a verb ends with a short vowel and a consonant, we double the consonant before adding the 'ing', 'ed' or 'er'.

I hop. You hop.
We hop.

They hop.

He hops.

She hops.

We are hopping.

In the past (yesterday),
we hopped.

We are hoppers.

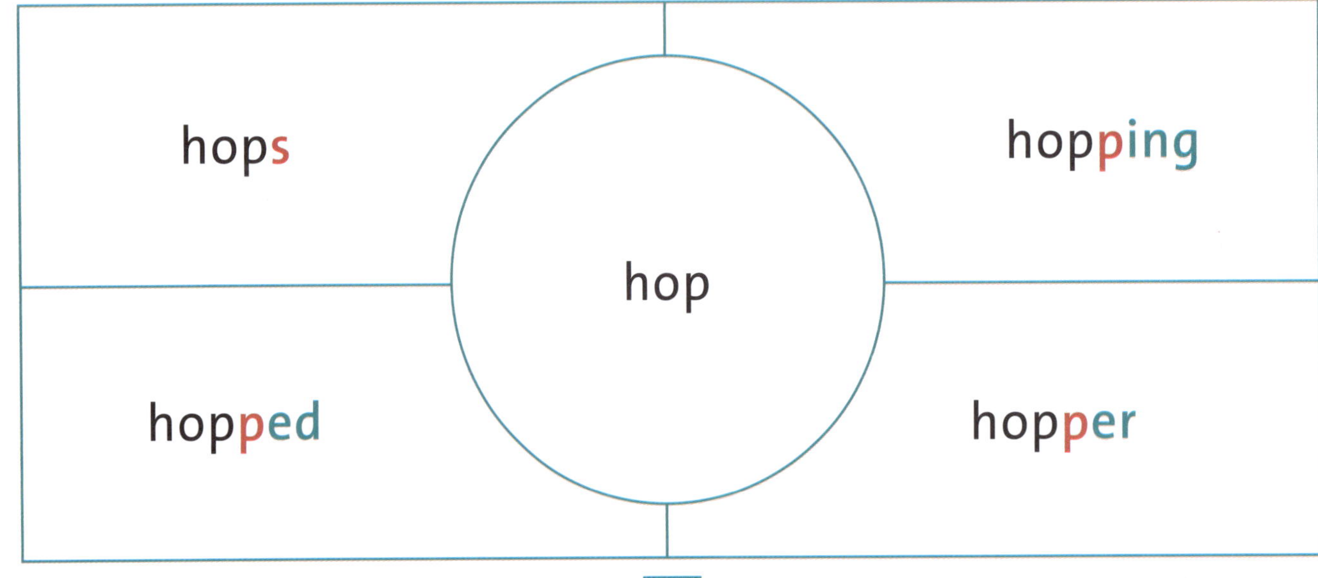

  ISBN: 9781925726367

Word families: verbs — s/ed/ing/er

Read the words. Complete the table by adding the endings to the words. The first one is done for you. Remember to double the final consonant before adding 'ing', 'ed' or 'er'.
These verbs are *regular* verbs. Their past tense verbs end with 'ed' after the final consonant is doubled.

Verb	s	ing	ed	er
hum	hums	humming	hummed	hummer
grab				
jog				
plan				
sip				
hop				
clap				
shop				
chat				
bat				
skid				
nod				

Read the list of words ending with 'ed'. Did you remember?
When verbs end with a voiced consonant; for example, m, b, g and n, the letters 'ed' make the 'd' sound.
When the verbs end with an unvoiced consonant; for example, p the letters 'ed' make the 't' sound.
When the verbs end with a 't' or a 'd', the letters 'ed' make the 'ed' sound.

Some verbs are *irregular* verbs. Their past tense words do not follow the 'ed' pattern.
Read the words. Complete the table. The past tense is completed for you.

Verb	s	ing	(past)	er
run			ran	
shut			shut	
swim			swam	
sit			sat	
cut			cut	

  ISBN: 9781925726367

Word families: adjectives

Now you know that endings are used to change the tense or form of verbs.
In this lesson, you will learn that endings can be added to adjectives (describing words) to compare things.
We usually use 'er' to compare two things, and 'est' to compare three or more things.

tall		
tall	taller	
tall	taller	tallest

  ISBN: 9781925726367

Word families: adjectives — er/est

Adding 'er' and 'est' to adjectives follows the same rules as adding the endings to verbs.

If the adjective has a long vowel or ends in two consonants, the endings are simply added to the words; for example: small, smaller, smallest.

If the adjective ends with a short vowel and one consonant, the final consonant is doubled before adding the ending; for example: big, bigger, biggest.

If the adjective ends with an 'e', we leave the 'e' off the end before adding the ending; for example: large, larger, largest.

Complete the table below by filling in the adjectives and the words that compare 2 or more than 2 things. Remember the rules about doubling the final consonant or leaving off the 'e'.

The first one is done for you.

Adjective	Compare 2	Compare 3+
grand	grander	grandest
fresh		
	higher	
		strongest
	kinder	
quick		
	thinner	
hot		
		flattest
	sadder	
fit		
brave		
		ripest
	wiser	
		cutest
nice		

These words do not follow the same pattern:

good	better	best
bad	worse	worst

  ISBN: 9781925726367

⋆ Unit 4 Review ⋆

Word families: verbs — s, ing, ed, er

Look at the picture. Read the story. Write the correct form of the words in brackets to tell what the children ***are doing now***.

1. The children are ______ ______ ______ ______ ______ ______ (have) fun at the park.
2. The tallest boy is ______ ______ ______ ______ ______ ______ ______ ______ (throw) a ball into a hoop.
3. The shortest boy is ______ ______ ______ ______ ______ ______ ______ ______ (bounce) a ball on the ground.
4. The boy with blonde hair is ______ ______ ______ ______ ______ ______ ______ (kick) a ball.
5. Three girls are ______ ______ ______ ______ ______ ______ ______ (play) with a skipping rope.
6. Two taller girls are ______ ______ ______ ______ ______ ______ ______ (turn) the rope.
7. The smallest girl is ______ ______ ______ ______ ______ ______ ______ (jump) the rope.

Now write the correct form of the words in brackets to tell what the children ***did yesterday***.

8. Yesterday, the children ______ ______ ______ (have) fun at the park.
9. The tallest boy ______ ______ ______ ______ ______ (throw) a ball into a hoop.
10. The shortest boy ______ ______ ______ ______ ______ ______ ______ (bounce) a ball on the ground.
11. The boy with blonde hair ______ ______ ______ ______ ______ ______ (kick) a ball.
12. Three girls ______ ______ ______ ______ ______ ______ (play) with a skipping rope.
13. Two taller girls ______ ______ ______ ______ ______ ______ (turn) the rope.
14. The smallest girl ______ ______ ______ ______ ______ ______ (jump) the rope.

  ISBN: 9781925726367

Word endings: adjectives — er, est

Look at the pictures in the boxes. Write the correct form of the word to compare the images.

large

light

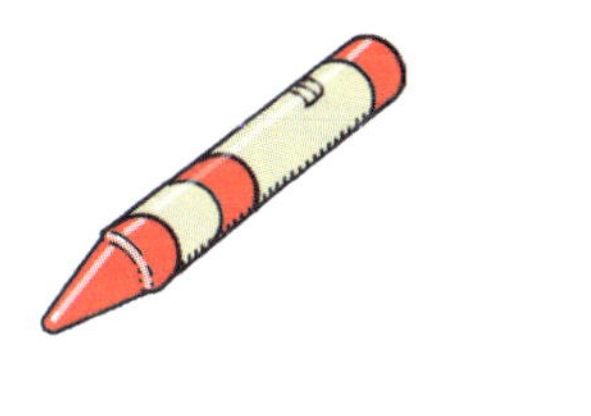

young

Write and draw.

Draw your own pictures in the boxes. Write the correct form of the word to compare the images you drew.

tall

old

  ISBN: 9781925726367

High Frequency Words — Unit 4

Here are some high frequency words to learn by sight.

live	middle	yesterday	any
again	don't	today	other

Reading and Comprehension

Read the story.

The Grass is Greener

Three goats lived on a hill where there was a lot of green grass to eat.

One day when they were munching grass, the smallest goat said, "Look over there. That grass is greener than ours. Can we go there?"

The biggest goat said, "It is not safe. A mean troll lives under the bridge. She eats goats."

"We are stronger and braver than any old troll," bragged the middle goat. "Come on."

The goats trotted down to the bridge.

The smallest goat went first. As he was crossing, the bridge started shaking.

"Don't eat me. My bigger brother is coming," he called, running away fast.

When the next brother crossed, the bridge started shaking again.

He ran away faster, shouting, "The biggest goat is coming!"

The biggest goat stomped across the bridge. He was so big, and the bridge was so weak, that it started breaking up. He jumped off just in time.

"You tricked us," said the middle goat. "There was no troll."

"But the bridge was not safe," said the biggest goat.

"Look over there," said the smallest goat. "That grass is the greenest of all."

  ISBN: 9781925726367

Tick the correct answer.

1. Where did the goats live?
   - ☐ a. On a hill
   - ☐ b. Under a bridge
   - ☐ c. With a troll
   - ☐ d. Where there is no grass
2. Why did the biggest goat say the bridge was not safe?
   - ☐ a. It was broken
   - ☐ b. It was too far
   - ☐ c. A troll lived there
   - ☐ d. The grass was green
3. Why did the goats cross the bridge?
   - ☐ a. To scare the troll
   - ☐ b. To get to the greener grass
   - ☐ c. To fix the bridge
   - ☐ d. To break the bridge
4. The middle goat said the goats were
   - ☐ a. Big and strong
   - ☐ b. Big and brave
   - ☐ c. Strong and brave
   - ☐ d. Little but brave
5. What gave the smallest goat a fright?
   - ☐ a. The troll jumped out.
   - ☐ b. His brother shouted.
   - ☐ c. The bridge started shaking.
   - ☐ d. The bridge was too far.
6. Did a mean troll live under the bridge?
   - ☐ a. Yes
   - ☐ b. No
   - ☐ c. Not sure
7. Do you think the grass over there was greener?
   - ☐ a. Yes
   - ☐ b. No
   - ☐ c. Not sure
8. Why did the bridge break?
   - ☐ a. The troll jumped on it.
   - ☐ b. The smallest goat jumped on it.
   - ☐ c. It was weak.
   - ☐ d. It was weak and the goats were big.

Write the answers to these questions in sentences.

9. Who crossed the bridge first?

   ____

10. What happened to the bridge when the goats crossed it?

   ____

Choose words from the box to complete each sentence.

strongest fastest dances better having played helping

1. Your work is good but mine is __ __ __ __ __ __.
2. Jeb got a badge for running __ __ __ __ __ __ __ in the race.
3. Yesterday, we __ __ __ __ __ __ on the swings at the park.
4. The __ __ __ __ __ __ __ __ __ man in the world can lift up a car.
5. I like __ __ __ __ __ __ __ my teacher get the balls for sport.
6. My little sister __ __ __ __ __ __ on the stage with her class.
7. The children are __ __ __ __ __ __ a good time at the beach.

Syllables

Now we will learn to decode and spell other words with more than one syllable. A syllable is a beat. If a word has more than one vowel sound, it has more than one syllable. The number of vowel sounds tells you the number of syllables. Every syllable has a vowel.
First, we will learn to decode two-syllable words with double consonants. The syllables break between the consonants. Decode each syllable as if they were separate words.

Say the names of the pictures. Colour the pictures with two syllables.

  ISBN: 9781925726367

Syllables: double consonants

Read the words. Draw lines to match them to the pictures.

	mattress		muffin
	butter		dinner
	rabbit		puppy
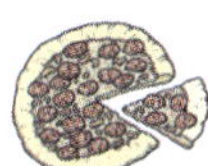	rubbish		balloon
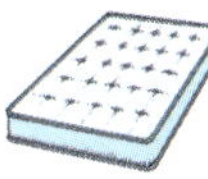	pizza		bubble

Look at these words. Show how to break them into syllables.

little = ____ + ____		hiccup = ____ + ____
funny = ____ + ____		happen = ____ + ____
yellow = ____ + ____		happy = ____ + ____
cotton = ____ + ____		apple = ____ + ____
riddle = ____ + ____		letter = ____ + ____

Look at the pictures. Write the words. Break them into syllables to help.

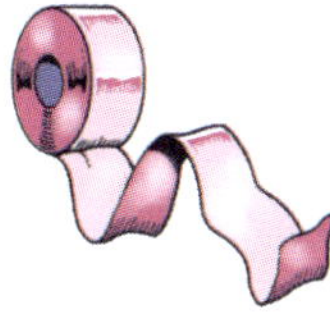 ______________________

 ______________________

 ______________________

 ______________________

  ISBN: 9781925726367

Syllables

Now we will learn to decode two-syllable words with two or more consonants that are not the same. Remember, every syllable has a vowel. As for double consonants, the syllables break between the consonants, but do not break between the consonants in digraphs or blends. Decode each syllable as if they were separate words.

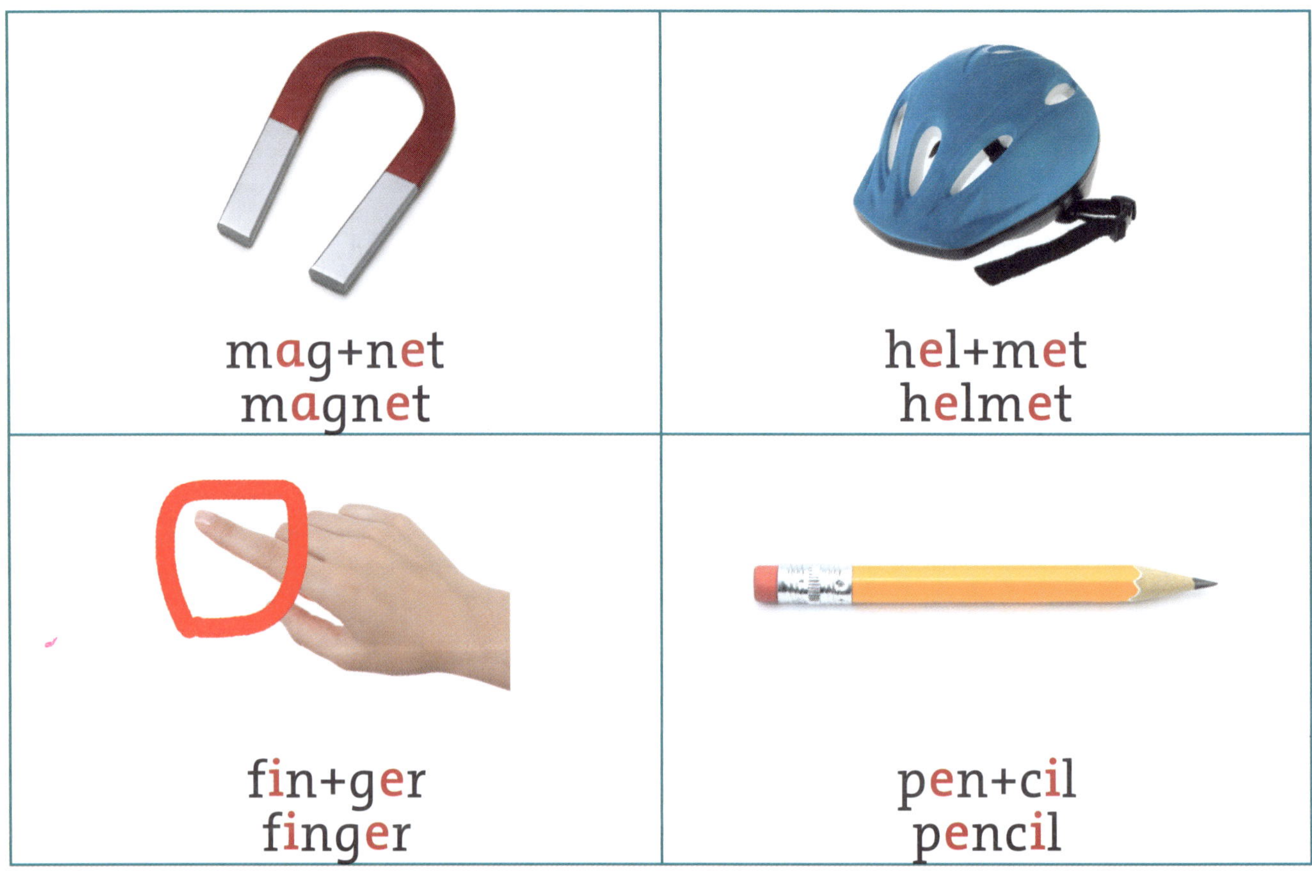

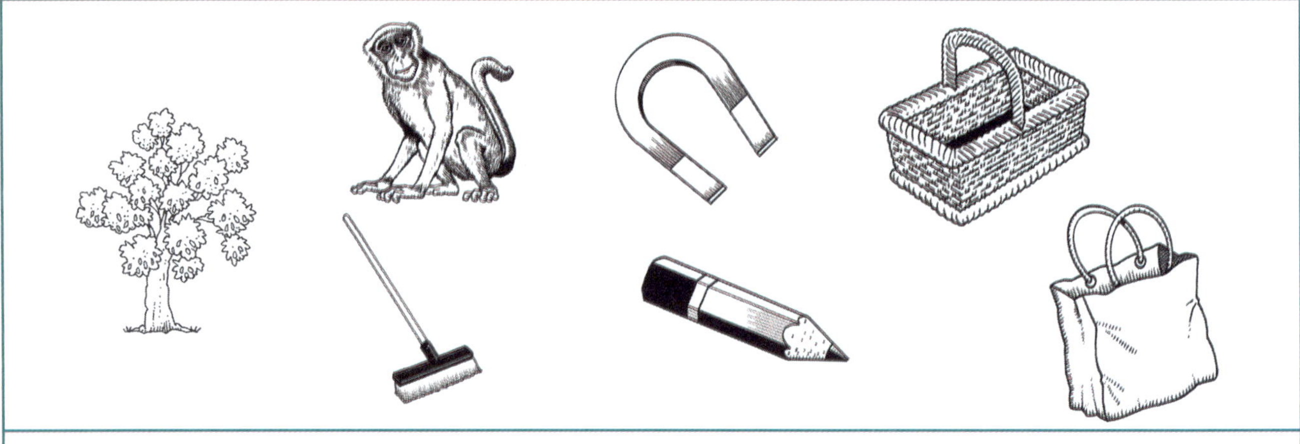

Say the names of the pictures. Colour the pictures with two syllables.

  ISBN: 9781925726367

Syllables: two or more consonants

Read the words. Draw lines to match them to the pictures.

	picnic		cactus
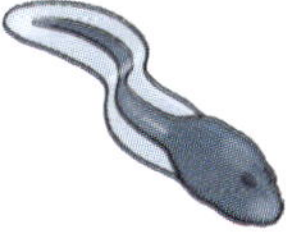	monkey		basket
	tadpole		trumpet
	doctor		pencil

Look at these words. Show how to break them into syllables. Remember, do not split consonant digraphs or blends.

timber = ____ + ____ pumpkin = ____ + ____

number = ____ + ____ winter = ____ + ____

after = ____ + ____ pretzel = ____ + ____

plastic = ____ + ____ reptile = ____ + ____

problem = ____ + ____ mistake = ____ + ____

Look at the pictures. Write the words. Break them into syllables to help.

 ____________________  ____________________

 ____________________  ____________________

  ISBN: 9781925726367

Syllables

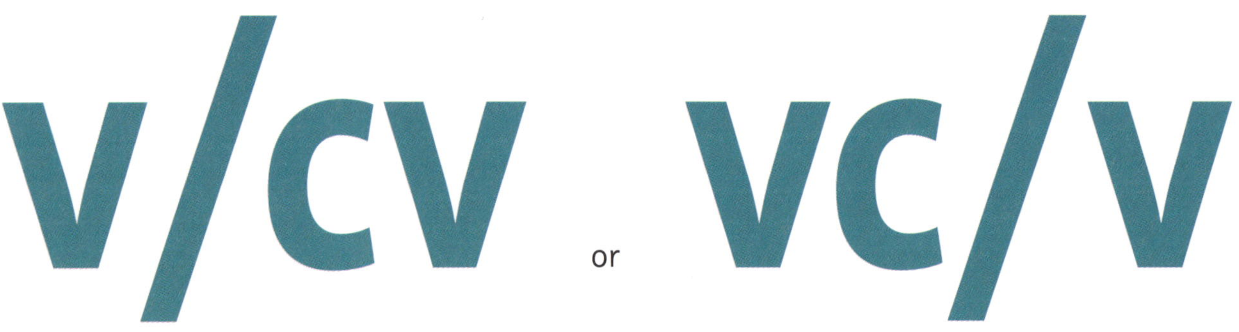

Now we will learn to decode two-syllable words in which one of the syllables ends or starts with a vowel. Remember, every syllable has a vowel. Remember also, that we do not break consonant digraphs or blends.
Usually, we break the syllables before the consonant if the first vowel sound is long as in 'cartoon'. Usually, we break the syllables after the consonant if the first vowel sound is short as in bucket. Decode each syllable as if they were separate words.

Say the names of the pictures. Colour the pictures with two syllables.

  ISBN: 9781925726367

Syllables: two or more consonants

Read the words. Draw lines to match them to the pictures.

	petal	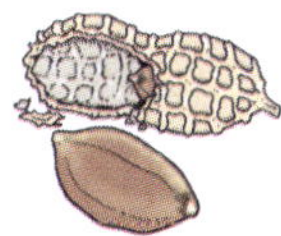	turkey
	cabin		peanut
	turtle		baby
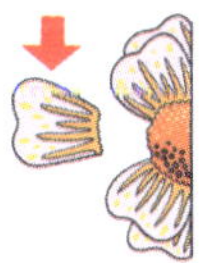	dragon		garden

Look at these words. Show how to break them into syllables.
Remember, do not split consonant digraphs or blends.

tonic = ____ + ____ season = ____ + ____

father = ____ + ____ pilot = ____ + ____

about = ____ + ____ scooter = ____ + ____

termite = ____ + ____ rocket = ____ + ____

human = ____ + ____ cookie = ____ + ____

Look at the pictures. Write the words. Break them into syllables to help.

 ________________  ________________

 ________________  ________________

 © PASCAL PRESS ISBN: 9781925726367

Syllables: 3 or more syllables

Now that you can decode two-syllable words, you can decode words with more than two syllables. Remember that every syllable has a vowel. If you find the vowels, you can find the syllables.

 but+ter+fly butterfly	 cat+er+pill+ar caterpillar
 croc+o+dile crocodile	 el+e+phant elephant

Say the names of the pictures. Write the number of syllables in the circles.

  ISBN: 9781925726367

Syllables: three or more syllables

Read the words. Draw lines to match them to the pictures.

 telephone

 vegetables

 telescope

 cucumber

 aquarium

 triangle

 binoculars

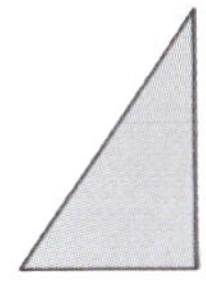 calculator

Look at these words. Underline the vowels. Remember some vowels are digraphs and trigraphs with two or three letters.
Show how to break the words into syllables. Write the number of syllables Remember, do not split consonant digraphs or blends. The first one is done for you.

con/so/nant 3

hippopotamus 

tomorrow 

macaroni 

suddenly 

important 

photograph 

yesterday 

Look at the pictures. Write the words. Break them into syllables to help.

 ____________________

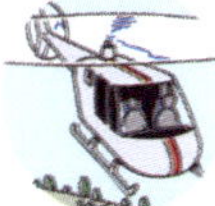 ____________________

 ____________________

 ____________________

  ISBN: 9781925726367

★ Unit 5 Review ★

Look at the words. Circle the vowels. Write the number of syllables in the word.
Write each syllable separately. Read the word. Draw a picture to illustrate the word. The first one is done for you.

Circle the vowels	How many syllables	Separate the syllables	Draw a picture
octopus	3	oc + to + pus	
peanut			
chocolate			
gorilla			
trumpet			
kangaroo			
dolphin			

  ISBN: 9781925726367

Revision Syllables

Read the words in the box. Count the syllables. Write the words in the correct part of the table.

shark wombat echidna platypus kitten carpenter
dragon insect branch playful cauliflower plastic
escalator cloud animal cupboard finishing
fantastic environment

One syllable	Two syllables	Three syllables	Four syllables

Choose a word from the table above to complete these sentences.

1. At the shopping centre, people go from one floor to another on an ____ ____ ____ ____ ____ ____ ____ ____ ____.
2. A ____ ____ ____ ____ ____ ____ is a baby cat.
3. A ____ ____ ____ ____ ____ ____ ____ ____ ____ ____ ____ is a type of vegetable.
4. Both the echidna and the ____ ____ ____ ____ ____ ____ ____ ____ are Australian marsupials.
5. A ____ ____ ____ ____ ____ ____ ____ ____ ____ is someone who works with wood.
6. A ____ ____ ____ ____ ____ ____ is a mythical creature that breathes fire.
7. We look after the ____ ____ ____ ____ ____ ____ ____ ____ ____ ____ ____ when we put our rubbish in the bin.
8. The crowd cheered because they thought the show was ____ ____ ____ ____ ____ ____ ____ ____ ____.

  ISBN: 9781925726367

Reading and Comprehension

Read the report.

Australian sea turtles

Six species of sea turtles live in Australian waters. Nearly all of them are endangered. All are protected.

Danger for sea turtles

Most threats to sea turtles are caused by people.

Rubbish is a hazard for sea turtles. If they swallow it, they can die. When rubbish is left lying around, it can get washed down the waterways. It can get blown by the wind into the ocean.

Turtles are often injured in fishing and boating accidents. They might get caught in nets or tangled in fishing lines. Some are hit by boats and other watercraft.

Sometimes the turtles' nests and eggs are destroyed by vehicles driving on the beach. When they do hatch, the young hatchlings can have difficulty finding their way to the water.

Help sea turtles

You can help sea turtles when you:

- Put all your rubbish in the bin.
- Pick up rubbish you see on the beach.
- Be mindful of sea turtle nests when visiting nesting beaches.
- Refuse to buy items made of turtle shell.
- Learn about sea turtles and organisations that help them.

  ISBN: 9781925726367

Write the answers to these questions in sentences.

1. How many species of sea turtles live in Australian waters?

   ____

2. How many of Australian sea turtles are protected?

   ____

3. Why is rubbish a hazard for sea turtles?

   ____

4. What happens to rubbish if it is left lying around?

   ____

5. How can fishing be harmful to turtles?

   ____

6. How do boats and other watercraft injure sea turtles?

   ____

7. What are some other watercraft you know?

   ____

8. Why are vehicles driving on the beach a danger to turtles?

   ____

9. What are baby turtles called?

   ____

10. What is one thing you can do to help save sea turtles?

    ____

There are 10 words with 3 or more syllables in the report. Can you find them all? Write them on these lines.

______________ ______________

______________ ______________

______________ ______________

______________ ______________

______________ ______________

  ISBN: 9781925726367

Silent letters

wh/wr

Use this QR code to watch and listen to the **letter WH/WR** sound cards below

You already know that the letters 'wh' spell the sound 'w' as in whale. The 'h' is silent.
Now you will learn that the letters 'wr' spell the sound 'r' as in write. The letter 'w' is silent.

 **wh**ale	 **wh**eel
 **wr**ite	 **wr**eath

Say the names of the pictures. Colour the picture that begin with the **w** sound. Circle the picture that start with the **r** sound.

Silent letters: wh/wr

In each of these words the 'h' is silent. The letters 'wh' spell the 'w' sound. Read the words. Underline or highlight the letters that spell the 'w' sound.

wh	whale	wheel	what	when
white	why	wheat	whelk	where
which	whip	whippet	whirl	whisk
whisker	whisper	whiff	whim	while

In each of these words the 'w' is silent. The letters 'wr' spell the 'r' sound. Read the words. Underline or highlight the letters that spell the 'r' sound.

Sometimes the letters 'wh' spell the 'h' sound and the 'w' is silent as in:
whole who
whose whom

wr	wrench	wreath	wrist	write
writer	wrote	writing	wreck	wren
wring	wrung	wrap	wrapper	wrong

Read the words. Draw lines to match them to the pictures.

whale

wheel

whip

whisk

wrench

wreath

wrist

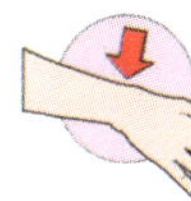
writing

Choose a word from the boxes above to complete these sentences.

1. It is hard to hear when you _ _ _ _ _ _ _ in my ear.
2. I like to have a chicken and salad _ _ _ _ for lunch.
3. The little _ _ _ _ _ clouds floated across the sky.
4. We _ _ _ _ _ in our books after lunch.
5. The wagon crashed when the _ _ _ _ _ fell off.
6. I got all my sums right. I did not get any _ _ _ _ _.

  ISBN: 9781925726367

Silent letters

gn/kn

Use this QR code to watch and listen to the **letter GN/KN** sound cards below

You already know that the 'h' in whale and the 'w' in write are silent letters. Now you will learn about some other silent letters. These silent letters usually occur at the beginning of words. In these words the 'g' and the 'k' are silent.

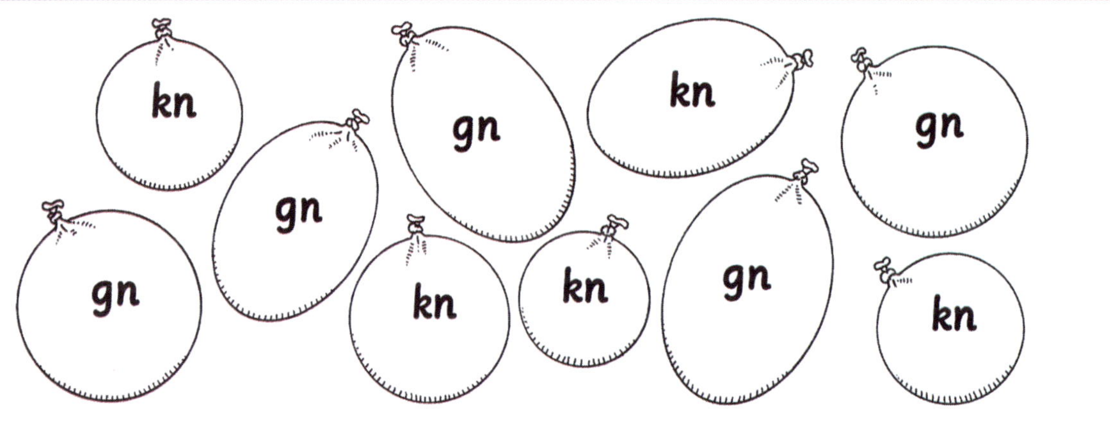

Look at the balloons. Colour the balloons with the letters **gn** green. Colour the balloons with the letters **kn** blue. Say **n** as you colour each balloon.

Silent letters: gn/kn

In each of these words the 'g' is silent. The letters 'gn' spell the 'n' sound. Read the words. Underline or highlight the letters that spell the 'n' sound. Circle the silent letter.

gn	gnome	gnu	gnash	gnaw
gnocchi	gnat	gnarl	sign	design

In each of these words the 'k' is silent. The letters 'kn' spell the 'n' sound. Read the words. Underline or highlight the letters that spell the 'n' sound. Circle the silent letter.

kn	knight	knife	know	knew
knee	knob	knit	knitting	knickers
knock	knot	knave	knead	knack

Read the words. Draw lines to match them to the pictures.

gnome

gnu

gnat

sign

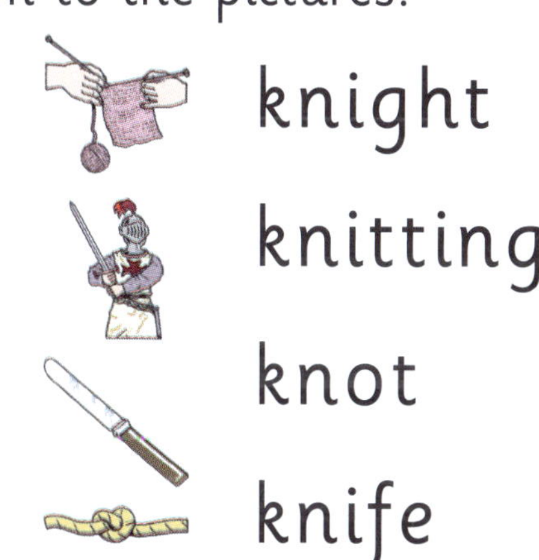

knight

knitting

knot

knife

Choose a word from the boxes above to complete these sentences.

1. The little mouse tried to ____ ____ ____ ____ through the rope.
2. I ____ ____ ____ ____ how to read and write all my words.
3. The ____ ____ ____ ____ on the road said there was no left turn.
4. My shoe laces had a ____ ____ ____ ____ in them.
5. The garden ____ ____ ____ ____ ____ had a pointy red cap.
6. The little boy grazed his ____ ____ ____ ____ when he fell over.
7. A ____ ____ ____ ____ is a tiny insect that bites.
8. I like to have a ____ ____ ____ ____ of butter on my corn.

  ISBN: 9781925726367

Silent letters

h/t/w

Use this QR code to watch and listen to the **letter H/T/W** sound cards below

Some words have silent letters in the middle. The letters 'h', 't' and 'w' are sometimes silent.

 ghost	 school
 castle	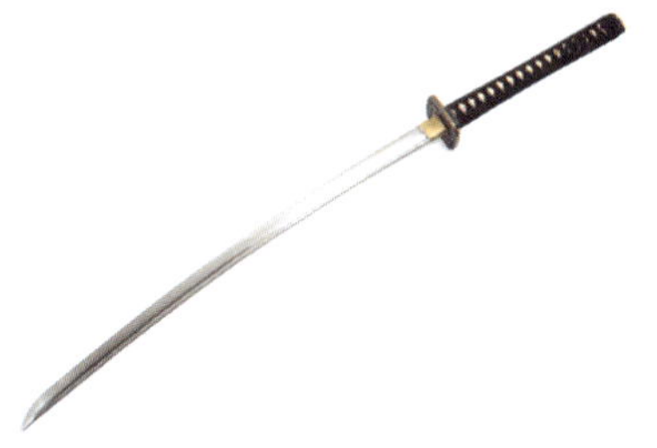 sword

Look at the pictures. Read the words. Each of the words has a silent letter. Circle the silent letter.

whale

ballet

1 2 3 4 5

2

two

sword

knight

  ISBN: 9781925726367

Silent letters: h/t/w

In each of these words the 'h' is silent. Read the words.
Circle the silent letter.

silent h	ghost	rhyme	mechanic	rhythm
school	scheme	honest	hour	whale
Christmas	chord	chrome	echo	chemical

In each of these words the 't' is silent. Read the words.
Circle the silent letter.

silent t	castle	Christmas	butcher	fasten
listen	often	nestle	ballet	soften

Each of these words has a silent letter. The silent letter is highlighted.
Read the words.

sword	answer	two	could	folk

Read the words. Draw lines to match them to the pictures.
Circle the silent letters.

 school

 mechanic

 castle

 listen

Choose a word from the boxes above to complete these sentences.

1. We always ___ ___ ___ ___ ___ ___ our seat belts when we go in the car.
2. I like learning how to read at ___ ___ ___ ___ ___ ___.
3. I can ___ ___ ___ ___ ___ ___ all the questions on the test.
4. I am always ___ ___ ___ ___ ___ ___ and tell the truth.
5. We ___ ___ ___ ___ ___ ___ to the coach so we know what to do.
6. We buy our meat at the ___ ___ ___ ___ ___ ___ ___ shop.

  ISBN: 9781925726367

Silent letters

b

Use this QR code to watch and listen to the **letter B** sound cards below

Some words have silent letters at the end. The letter 'b' is sometimes silent at the end of a word, usually when it follows the letter 'm'.

Look at the pictures. Read the words. Each of the words has a silent letter. Circle the silent letter.

  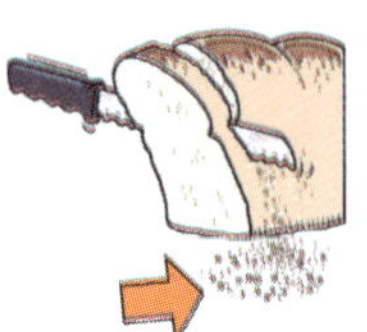 

thumb comb lamb crumbs climber

  ISBN: 9781925726367

Silent letters: b

In each of these words the 'b' is silent. Read the words.
Circle the silent letter.

silent b	thumb	comb	bomb	lamb
climb	crumb	dumb	limb	numb
tomb	plumb	plumber	climber	
debt	doubt			

Read the words. Draw lines to match them to the pictures.
Circle the silent letters.

 thumb

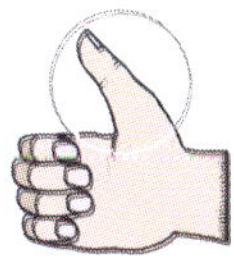 crumbs

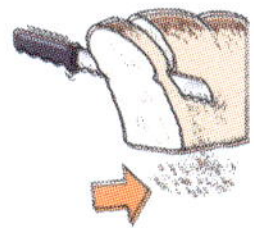 climber

 comb

 lamb

 bomb

Choose a word from the box above to complete these sentences.

1. I can ____ ____ ____ ____ ____ the highest wall at the park.
2. The little boy hit his ____ ____ ____ ____ ____ with the hammer.
3. Mum told me to ____ ____ ____ ____ my hair before I went out.
4. He was telling the truth. I had no ____ ____ ____ ____ ____.
5. When we went to the farm we fed a baby ____ ____ ____ ____.
6. My mouth was ____ ____ ____ ____ after I went to the dentist.

Read these words. Circle the words with a silent 'b'.

bat lamb bomb cab
debt web climb
comb boy numb

  ISBN: 9781925726367

⋆ Unit 6 Review ⋆

Silent letters

Read the words. Draw lines to match them to the pictures.
Circle the silent letters.

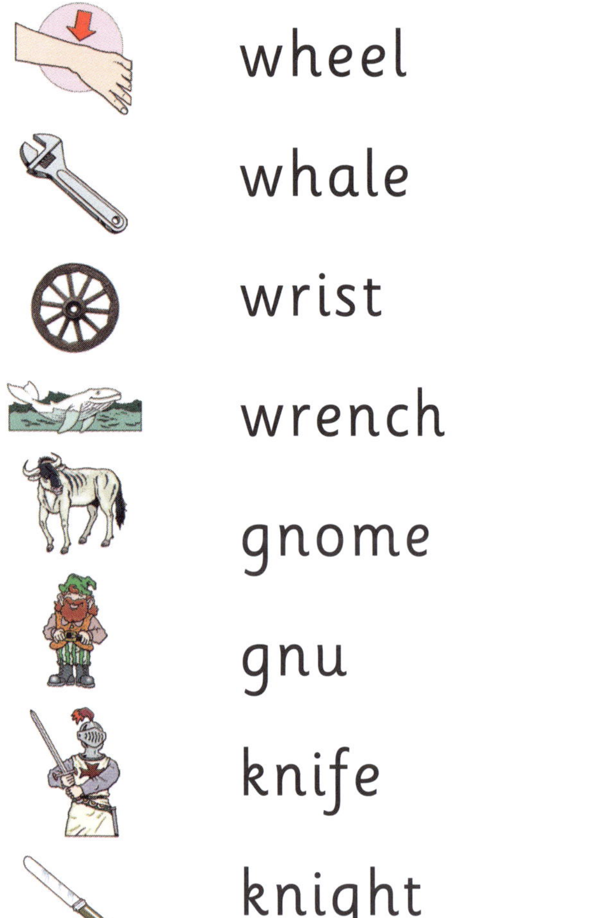

wheel

whale

wrist

wrench

gnome

gnu

knife

knight

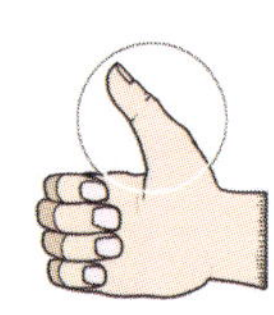

ghost

school

sign

thumb

bomb

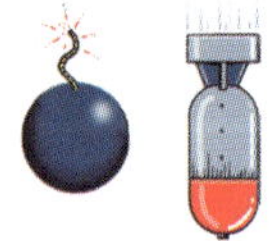

gnat

Choose the correct word

Look at the pictures. Read the pairs of words. Circle the correct word.

comb come	homb home	knot not
goast ghost	sawd sword	wreath reath
nife knife	bomb bomm	nat gnat

  ISBN: 9781925726367

Silent letters

Read the words in the box. Circle the silent letter. Write the words in the correct part of the table.

wheat wrist gnat knot comb gnaw
honest crumb wreck climb sign
kneel wrong wheel knew knock doubt
gnome school write

Silent h	Silent w	Silent k	Silent g	Silent b

Choose a word from the table above to complete these sentences.

1. We took the ____ ____ ____ ____ ____ turn and ended up lost.
2. We all got a fright when there was a loud ____ ____ ____ ____ ____ on the door.
3. The farmer's ____ ____ ____ ____ ____ was ripe and ready to harvest.
4. I ____ ____ ____ ____ the answers to all the questions.
5. The teacher told us to ____ ____ ____ ____ ____ our names on our books.
6. I saw a kangaroo on the way to ____ ____ ____ ____ ____ ____ today.
7. There is a ____ ____ ____ ____ in the window saying the shop is closed.
8. I tied a ____ ____ ____ ____ in the rope so it wouldn't come loose.
9. I always ____ ____ ____ ____ my hair when I get up in the morning.
10. We watched the boy ____ ____ ____ ____ ____ right to the top of the ladder.

  ISBN: 9781925726367

Reading and Comprehension

Read the report.

Planning a story

When you write a story, you have to decide:

- Who will the story be about?
- When and where will the story take place?
- What will happen and why?
- How will it end?

I could write a story about a boy who wants to be a knight.

He could use a knife as a pretend sword. No, that would be wrong. I doubt a boy would have a knife. Okay, no sword.

I know he will be a brave knight though. He will be honest too. He will make the garden gnome and the clay lamb come to life. They will be his troops and go on many quests together.

They could climb high mountains and follow signs to a castle. When they get there, they knock on the door.

Then what happens?

What if a ghost answers? That would be funny. Their faces would go white with fright.

Or maybe an old woman who is knitting a sweater answers the door.

Or a princess combing her hair.

Oh dear. I do not know how my story should end. What do you think?

  ISBN: 9781925726367

Write the answers to these questions in sentences.

1. Who will my story be about?

 ____

2. When do you think the story takes place?

 ____

3. Why would I not give the knight in my story a knife for a pretend sword?

 ____

4. What two words describe the knight?

 ____

5. What does the knight use for troops?

 ____

6. How does the knight find his way to the castle?

 ____

7. What does the knight do when he gets to the castle?

 ____

8. Why did I think the knight's face might go white?

 ____

9. Who do you think should open the door?

 ____

10. How do you think the story should end?

 ____

There are more than 20 different words with silent letters in the story. How many can you find? Circle them in the text, then write them on these lines.

________	________	________
________	________	________
________	________	________
________	________	________
________	________	________
________	________	________

Final Words

zh

Use this QR code to watch and listen to the **letter ZH** sound cards below

Now you know which letters are used to represent the most common sounds of the English language and can use that knowledge to decode words having two or more syllables.
In this unit you will learn some sounds that mostly occur in words of two or more syllables.

Look at the pictures. Say their names. Listen carefully. Some have the **sh** sound, some have the **z** sound and some have the **zh** sound. Write letters in the circle to tell what sounds you hear.

  ISBN: 9781925726367

Final Words: zh

Each of these words has the sound 'zh'. The letters that are used to spell the sound are coloured green. Read the words. Make the 'zh' sound when you see the green letters.

zh	treasure	measure	pleasure	casual
casualty	usual	usually	visual	exposure
television	Asia	vision	division	erosion
explosion	collision	inclusion		
beige	rouge	camouflage	collage	mirage
genre				
azure	seizure			

Read the words. Draw lines to match them to the pictures. Circle the letters that represent the 'zh' sound.

 treasure

 collage

 explosion

 television

 camouflage

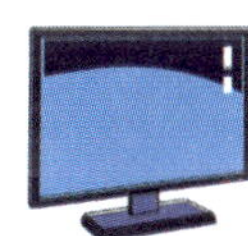 division

Choose a word from the box above to complete these sentences.

1. We ___ ___ ___ ___ ___ ___ ___ have fish and chips on Friday nights.
2. There was a big ___ ___ ___ ___ ___ ___ ___ ___ ___ at the quarry.
3. I like it when we do ___ ___ ___ ___ ___ ___ ___ in art lessons.
4. The thirsty man saw a ___ ___ ___ ___ ___ ___ when he was lost in the desert.
5. My grandmother wears glasses to assist her ___ ___ ___ ___ ___ ___.
6. Fairy tales are my favourite ___ ___ ___ ___ ___ to read.
7. The sky is a beautiful ___ ___ ___ ___ ___ blue today.
8. Dad lets us watch ___ ___ ___ ___ ___ ___ ___ ___ ___ ___ when we have finished our homework.

  ISBN: 9781925726367

Schwa sound

Words with two or more syllables have one or more stressed syllables and one or more unstressed syllables. The vowel in the unstressed syllable usually has the schwa sound.
While the schwa sound is represented by an upside-down e, you will not see that symbol in any written words. You will only see the letters that represent the vowel sounds: a, e, i, o, u and y.

Use this QR code to watch and listen to the **schwa** sound cards below

Look at the pictures. Read the words. Draw a line to separate the syllables. Circle the unstressed syllable.

rabbit

guitar

saucepan

dolphin

tractor

Schwa sound

Each of these words has the schwa sound. The letters that are used to spell the sound are coloured green. Read the words. Listen for the schwa sound when you see the green letters.

camel	butterfly	present	accident	silent
comma	difficult	salad	banana	vinyl
festival	enemy	item	pencil	zebra
balloon	button	dinosaur	calendar	support
focus	alphabet	camouflage	animal	wagon

Read the words. Draw lines to match them to the pictures. Circle the letters where you hear the schwa sound.

carrot
flower
wizard
octopus
helmet

panda
elephant
parrot
lemon
avocado

Choose a word from the box above to complete these sentences.

1. I asked my teacher for help when the work was ___ ___ ___ ___ ___ ___ ___ ___ ___.
2. T-Rex is my favourite ___ ___ ___ ___ ___ ___ ___ ___.
3. Dad always makes ___ ___ ___ ___ ___ ___ pancakes on Sundays.
4. The little boy cried when his ___ ___ ___ ___ ___ ___ ___ floated away.
5. We use letters of the ___ ___ ___ ___ ___ ___ ___ ___ to spell our words.
6. The blue whale is the largest ___ ___ ___ ___ ___ ___ that ever lived.
7. We count down the days until the holidays on the ___ ___ ___ ___ ___ ___ ___ ___.
8. It is better to be a friend than an ___ ___ ___ ___ ___.

  ISBN: 9781925726367

Word endings

y/le/tion

Use this QR code to watch and listen to the **letter Y/LE/TION** sound cards below

Now you will learn some common word endings for words with two or more syllables.

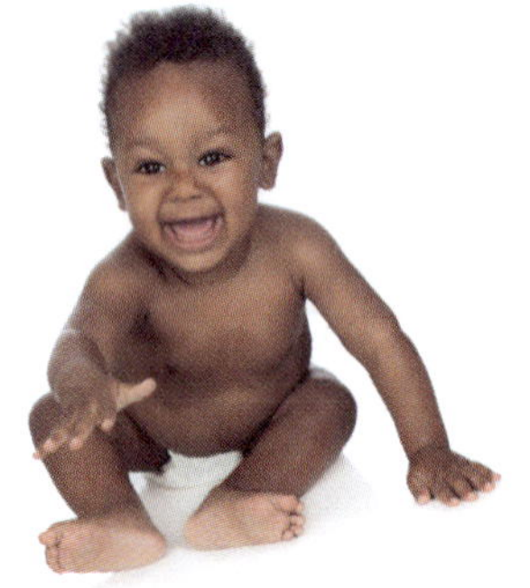 baby	 lady
 turtle	 bubble
 potion	 decoration

  ISBN: 9781925726367

Word endings: y/le/tion

Each of these words end with 'y' that has the long 'e' sound.
Read the words. Circle the 'y'.

y = ee	baby	lady	mummy	daddy
happy	funny	lovely	lucky	family
sticky	tiny	bunny	softly	energy

Each of these words end with 'le' that makes the 'l' sound. Read the words. Circle the 'le'.

le	turtle	bubble	whistle	table
cable	nibble	apple	marble	puddle
cycle	uncle	eagle	middle	example

Each of these words end with 'tion' that sounds like 'shun'. Read the words. Circle the 'tion'.

tion	potion	decoration	invitation	education
instruction	direction	vacation	operation	lotion
nation	emotion	solution	addition	caution

Read the words. Draw lines to match them to the pictures.

	potion		bicycle
	decoration		bunny
	apple		eagle
	marble		family

Choose a word from the box above to complete these sentences.

1. I gave my friends an __ __ __ __ __ __ __ __ __ __ to my party.
2. My whole __ __ __ __ __ __ likes going to the beach for holidays.
3. The computer would not work as the __ __ __ __ __ was not plugged in.
4. We had to speak __ __ __ __ __ __ so we would not wake the baby.
5. I woke up in the __ __ __ __ __ __ of the night when it was storming.
6. The sign said to use __ __ __ __ __ __ __ where the men were working.

  ISBN: 9781925726367

Compound Words

rainbow

Now you can read words with more than one syllable, you can read compound words. Compound words are words that are made by joining two smaller words together. You decode them by breaking the words into syllables the same way as you did before.

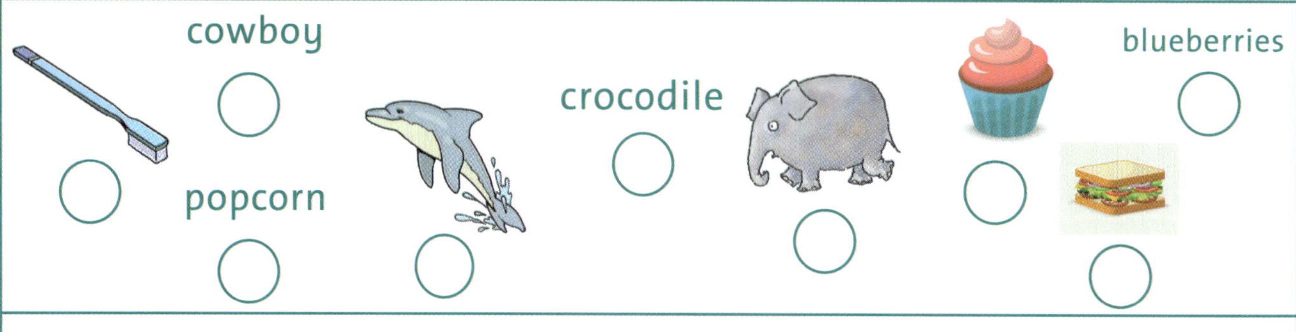

Look at the pictures or read the words. Place a tick (✓) in the circle if it is a compound word.

  ISBN: 9781925726367

Compound Words

Each of these words is a compound word. Read the words. Draw a | to separate the words. The first one is done for you.

Compound words	rain | bow	birthday
homework	airport	airplane
somewhere	teamwork	football
netball	hairbrush	network
backpack	notebook	scrapbook
cupcake	pancakes	whiteboard
snowman	outside	spaceship
butterfly	grandmother	grandfather
jellyfish	wheelbarrow	strawberry

Read the words. Draw lines to match them to the pictures. Draw a | to separate the words.

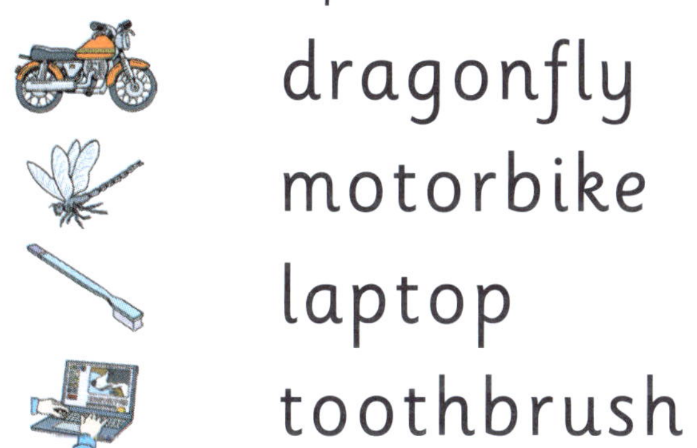

dragonfly

motorbike

laptop

toothbrush

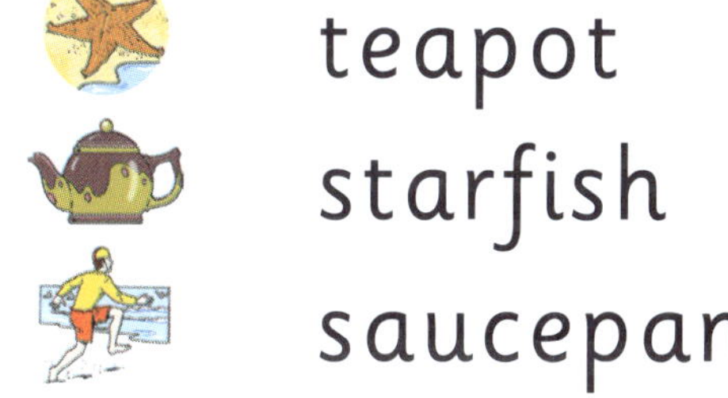

teapot

starfish

saucepan

lifeguard

Choose a word from the box above to complete these sentences.

1. I left my book ___ ___ ___ ___ ___ ___ ___ ___ ___ and now I can't find it.
2. I had a ___ ___ ___ ___ ___ ___ ___ ___ ___ ___ milkshake at the shops.
3. My ___ ___ ___ ___ ___ ___ ___ ___ ___ ___ ___ gave me some money for my birthday.
4. We saw a lot of ___ ___ ___ ___ ___ ___ ___ ___ ___ washed up on the sand at the beach.
5. Dad lets me watch television after I finish my ___ ___ ___ ___ ___ ___ ___ ___.
6. ___ ___ ___ ___ ___ ___ ___ ___ is important when we work together in groups.
7. I like going to the ___ ___ ___ ___ ___ ___ ___ to watch the planes land.

  ISBN: 9781925726367

⋆ Unit 7 Review ⋆

Zh/schwa sound/y/le/tion

Read the words. Draw lines to match them to the pictures.

 treasure

 button

 turtle

 potion

 television

 elephant

 whistle

 explosion

 direction

 castle

 marble

 eagle

 jelly

 family

Choose the correct word

Look at the pictures. Read the pairs of words. Circle the correct word.

treasure treazure	collizon collision	belloon balloon
salad saled	babee baby	bubble bubbl
lotion loshun	puddle puddl	ladie lady

  ISBN: 9781925726367

Compound words

Read the words in the boxes. Choose a word from the box on the left and match it with a word in the box on the right to make a compound word. Write the words and draw the pictures to illustrate the compound words you have made in the boxes below.

foot	space	super
dragon	back	cup
tool	spider	hair

pack	hero	web	ship
ball	cake	box	
brush	fly		

Choose one of your compound words from the table above to complete these sentences.

1. The pretty blue ___ ___ ___ ___ ___ ___ ___ ___ ___ hovered above the water.
2. The aliens arrived on Earth in a ___ ___ ___ ___ ___ ___ ___ ___ ___ .
3. I had a ___ ___ ___ ___ ___ ___ ___ for afternoon tea.
4. My grandmother gave me a new ___ ___ ___ ___ ___ ___ ___ ___ ___ for my birthday.
5. My favourite ___ ___ ___ ___ ___ ___ ___ ___ ___ is Batman.
6. There was a big ___ ___ ___ ___ ___ ___ ___ ___ ___ in the garden today.
7. We played with my ___ ___ ___ ___ ___ ___ ___ ___ at lunchtime today.
8. I took my football to school in my ___ ___ ___ ___ ___ ___ ___ ___.
9. My dad keeps his hammer in his ___ ___ ___ ___ ___ ___ ___.

  ISBN: 9781925726367

Reading and Comprehension

Read the report.

Summer Holidays

Every year, Jamie and his family stayed at the Beachside Vacation Park for the summer holidays. Jamie had fun because there were always other children to play with.

Jamie and his summertime friends would dive through waves and ride their bodyboards, pretending they were turtles and dolphins.

They would explore rock pools, finding starfish, whelks, crabs and other tiny creatures. Sometimes, they saw jellyfish and seaweed washed up on the seashore.

Just beyond the rock pools, there was a shipwreck. They had strict instructions to not go near it, and they didn't. But they would pretend it was a pirate ship and tell stories about pirate adventures.

One day, a man in a long black coat was peering at the shipwreck.

"Look," said Jamie. "A pirate. He's come for his treasure."

When the man spotted them, he hurried away.

"Let's follow him," said Jamie.

When they got to the top of the sand dune, the man had vanished.

"His footprints go in that direction," said Corey.

But the footprints soon disappeared too.

When the children told their parents about the pirate, they laughed.

"You children have such good imaginations," they said.

Write the answers to these questions in sentences.

1. In what season does the story take place?

____

2. Where does Jamie's family go for the summer holidays?

____

3. What is Jamie doing when he is pretending to be a turtle or a dolphin?

____

4. What are some of the things Jamie finds in the rock pools?

____

5. Where does Jamie see jellyfish and seaweed?

____

6. Where are Jamie and his friends not allowed to go?

____

7. Why do you think the children are not allowed to go to the shipwreck?

____

8. What do the children pretend the shipwreck is?

____

9. What is the name of Jamie's friend?

____

10. Do you think the man is a real pirate? Why do you think that?

____

There are 10 different compound words in the story. How many can you find? Circle them in the text, then write them on these lines.

______________ ______________

______________ ______________

______________ ______________

______________ ______________

______________ ______________

  ISBN: 9781925726367

★ Book 3 Revision ★

Decoding

Read the words. Draw lines to match them to the pictures.

	shark	shrimp	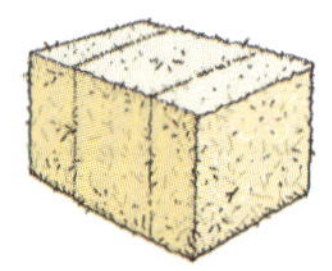
	bird	straw	
	worm	basket	
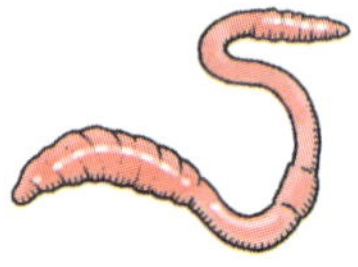	corn	gnome	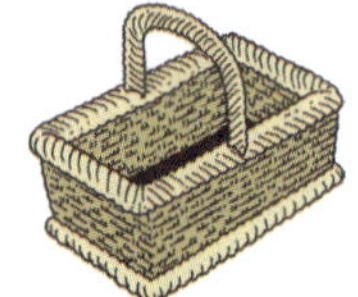
	ball	bomb	
	crown	treasure	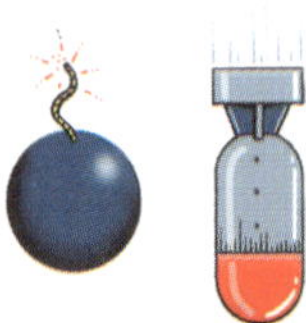
	coin	television	
	deer	whistle	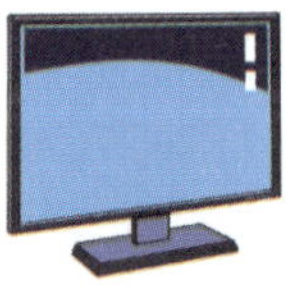
	fridge	jelly	
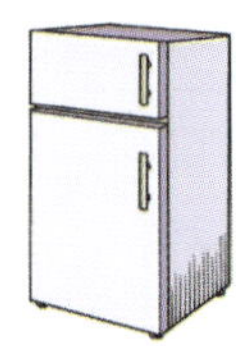	watch	watermelon	

  ISBN: 9781925726367

Spelling

Say the names of the pictures below. Write the letters that are missing from each word.

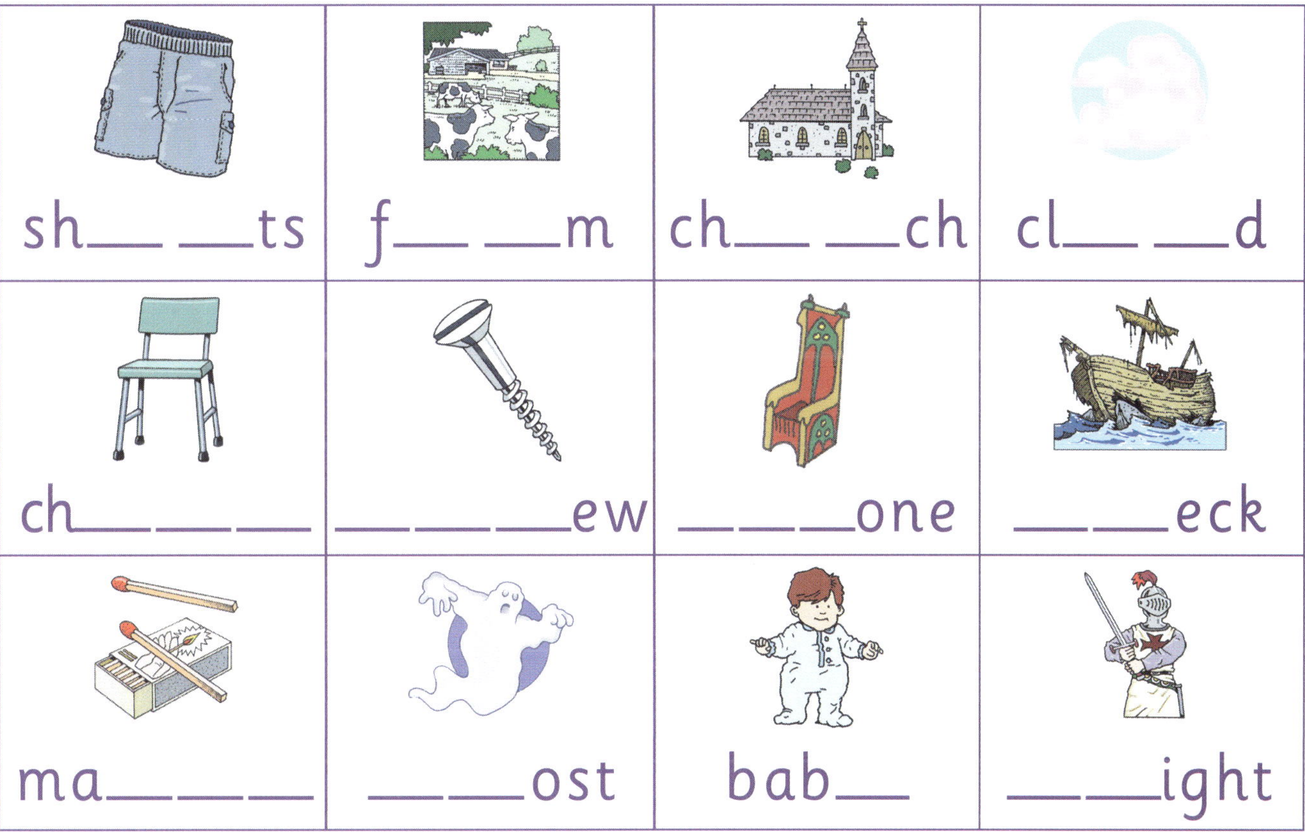

sh__ __ts	f__ __m	ch__ __ch	cl__ __d
ch______	______ew	_____one	_____eck
ma_____	_____ost	bab__	_____ight

Look at the pictures. Read the pairs of words. Circle the correct word.

curl cerl	bear beer	bridge brige	spits splits
comb come	sawd sword	nife knife	belloon balloon
hows house	jirarf giraffe	deer dear	boy buoy

  ISBN: 9781925726367

Choose words from the box to complete each sentence.

steer	badge	hatch	operation	knock
laugh	strongest	shrimp	mayor	pouch

1. When my Dad tickles me, he makes me ____ ____ ____ ____ ____.
2. I can ____ ____ ____ ____ ____ my bike safely through all these rocks
3. If all the eggs ____ ____ ____ ____ ____ we will have ten little ducklings.
4. The ____ ____ ____ ____ ____ ____ ____ ____ ____ man on Earth can lift up a car.
5. My mum had an ____ ____ ____ ____ ____ ____ ____ ____ ____ on her sore knee.
6. All of the people came out to listen to the town ____ ____ ____ ____ ____.
7. The school captains wear a ____ ____ ____ ____ ____ on their shirts.
8. The mother kangaroo has a joey in her ____ ____ ____ ____ ____.
9. A ____ ____ ____ ____ ____ ____ is similar to a prawn.
10. It is always polite to ____ ____ ____ ____ ____ on a door before entering.

Word families: verbs — s, ing, ed, er

Write the correct form of the verbs in brackets to complete the sentences

11. Yesterday, I ____ ____ ____ ____ my bike to school. (ride)
12. We are all ____ ____ ____ ____ ____ ____ ____ football after school. (play)
13. The ____ ____ ____ ____ ____ ____ of the competition will get a trophy. (win)
14. Mum ____ ____ ____ ____ ____ the broken door handle. (fix)
15. The little boy always ____ ____ ____ ____ ____ too loud. (talk)
16. Last year, my music teacher ____ ____ ____ ____ ____ ____ me to play the violin. (teach)
17. All the trains are ____ ____ ____ ____ ____ ____ ____ on time. (run)
18. Last week I ____ ____ ____ ____ four chapters of my book. (read)
19. My family ____ ____ ____ ____ ____ ____ ____ the video about shark last night. (watch)
20. We are ____ ____ ____ ____ ____ to visit my grandpa on Saturday. (g

  ISBN: 9781925726367

Word families: adjectives — er, est

Look at the pictures in the boxes. Write the correct form of the word to compare the images.

long

high

bright

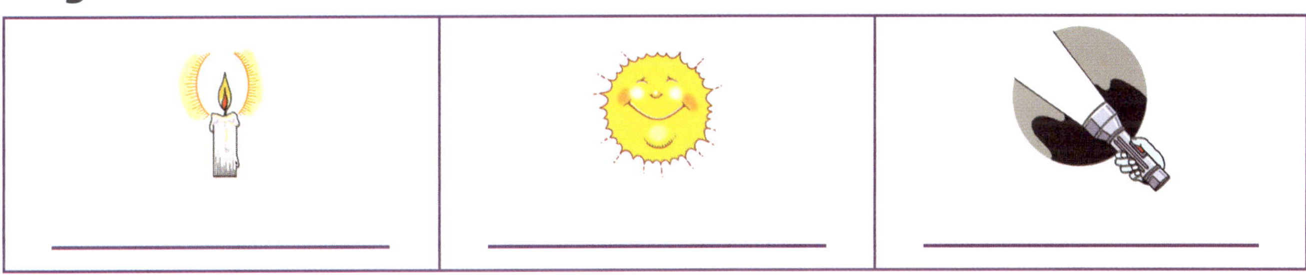

Syllables

Read the words in the box. Count the syllables. Write the words in the correct part of the table.

desk computer keyboard mouse tablet
laptop security cord program website
digital processor compatible internet bandwidth

One syllable	Two syllables	Three syllables	Four syllables

  ISBN: 9781925726367

Reading and Comprehension

Read the report.

The Internet

Nearly everyone has access to the internet these days. They can access it anywhere on mobile devices like phones, tablets and laptops. Desktop computers usually stay on the desk at home or in the workplace. Many people use the internet in their work. Others use it just for fun.

People can do almost anything on their devices.

When they are connected to the internet, they can:

- write emails
- look up information
- watch videos
- play games
- connect with others on social media
- do their shopping and banking

Children learn how to use computers at school.

They learn how to:

- use the keyboard, mouse and trackpad
- create and save files
- open and close programs
- access the internet safely
- download information from websites
- make sure the website and information are reliable

Even before they start school, many children use tablets and phones. They use them to play games and watch videos.

The internet is an important part of modern life. It is difficult to imagine life without it.

Write the answers to these questions in sentences.

1. What can people use to access the internet?

   ____

2. Where can people access the internet?

   ____

3. How is a mobile device different from a desktop computer?

   ____

4. List two things people can do when they are connected to the internet.

   a. ______________________________

   b. ______________________________

5. Where do children learn to use computers?

   ____

6. What do children learn to do with files?

   ____

7. What do children learn about accessing the internet?

   ____

8. What do children have to check when getting information from websites?

   ____

9. How do young children use the internet before they start school?

   ____

10. How important is the internet to modern life?

    ____

There are 10 different compound words in the story. How many can you find? Circle them in the text. Write them on these lines.

______________ ______________

______________ ______________

______________ ______________

______________ ______________

______________ ______________

  ISBN: 9781925726367

★A Selection of Decodable Words★

UNIT 1

ar	car	star	far	tart
mart	part	mark	shark	barn
farm	arm	bar	jar	start
park	sharp	scarf	chart	yard
laugh	heart	half	grass	giraffe
fast	past	glass		
er	fern	her	kerb	perch
verb	term	herd	herb	germ
verse	nerve	serve		
bird	fir	first	stir	twirl
shirt	skirt	dirt	squirt	girl
surf	turf	hurt	curl	turn
burn	church	fur	burst	nurse
purse	curve			
word	world	worth	work	worm
earn	search	pearl	heard	earth
learn	were			
or	fork	sport	storm	short
shorts	cork	port	north	torch
cord	corn	born	horn	form
more	sore	for	fore	four
store	force	score	snore	horse
shore	core	chores		
taught	caught	saw	paw	hawk
ball	fall	small	door	floor
talk	walk	sauce	your	board
war	bought	thought	fought	sure

  ISBN: 9781925726367

ow	cow	bow	brow	brown
frown	crown	down	clown	growl
gown	how	howl	now	prowl
town	owl	crowd		
out	house	loud	mouth	cloud
count	flour	proud	sound	bounce
sprout	shout	round	found	wound
mouse	trout	scout	pouch	south
plough	bough	drought		
oi	noise	coin	join	soil
oil	boil	void	coil	spoil
moist	joint	groin	voice	hoist
point	choice	oink	foil	toil
toy	ploy	joy	soy	coy
boy	buoy			
ear	fear	rear	hear	dear
near	gear	sear	tear	spear
clear	year	beard		
beer	deer	steer	cheer	veer
sheer	peer	sneer		
pier	fierce	weir	sphere	here
air	fair	lair	hair	pair
chair	chairs	flair		
bear	tear	pear	wear	
care	fare	share	mare	dare
bare	rare	hare	scare	spare
glare	square	flare	snare	stare
where	there	their	mayor	prayer

 © PASCAL PRESS ISBN: 9781925726367

tch	catch	hatch	patch	batch
match	fetch	sketch	itch	witch
snitch	ditch	pitch	stitch	watch
hutch				
dge	badge	edge	hedge	ridge
bridge	fridge	lodge	smudge	fudge
nudge	judge			
scr	scratch	script	scream	scribe
scrap	screw	scrub	screech	scram
scrape	screen			
str	stripe	strain	strong	strap
strand	stray	strip	street	stretch
strange	straight	strict	string	stress
struck	stream	strength	strike	straw

spr	spray	spree	sprig	spread
spring	sprain	sprout	sprite	sprawl
sprint	spruce	spry		

spl	splash	splat	splay	split
splosh	spleen	splint	splice	
shr	shrimp	shrine	shred	shrub
shrug	shrank	shrunk	shrink	shrewd
shrill	shrike	shroud	shriek	
thr	three	throw	threw	thread
throb	throat	thrust	thrill	throng
throne	thrush	through		

  ISBN: 9781925726367

wh	whale	wheel	what	when
white	why	wheat	whelk	where
which	whip	whippet	whirl	whisk
whisker	whisper	whiff	whim	while

wr	wrench	wreath	wrist	write
writer	wrote	writing	wreck	wren
wrap	wrapper	wrong		

gn	gnome	gnu	gnash	gnaw
gnocchi	gnat	gnarl	sign	design

kn	knight	knife	know	knew
knee	knob	knit	knitting	knickers
knock	knot	knave	knead	knack

silent h	ghost	rhyme	mechanic	rhythm
school	scheme	honest	hour	whale
Christmas	chord	chrome	echo	chemical

silent t	castle	Christmas	butcher	fasten
listen	often	nestle	ballet	soften

sword	answer	two	could	folk

silent b	thumb	comb	bomb	lamb
climb	crumb	dumb	limb	numb
tomb	plumb	plumber	climber	
debt	doubt			

  ISBN: 9781925726367

zh	treasure	measure	pleasure	casual
casualty	usual	usually	visual	exposure
television	Asia	vision	division	erosion
explosion	collision	inclusion		
beige	rouge	camouflage	collage	mirage
genre	azure	seizure		

y = ee	baby	lady	mummy	daddy
happy	funny	lovely	lucky	family
sticky	tiny	bunny	softly	energy

le	turtle	bubble	whistle	table
cable	nibble	apple	marble	puddle
cycle	uncle	eagle	middle	example

tion	potion	decoration	invitation	education
instruction	direction	vacation	operation	lotion
nation	emotion	solution	addition	caution

  ISBN: 9781925726367

★ High Frequency Words — Unit 1 ★

giraffe	half	heart	laugh	were
one	old	two	under	grass

★ High Frequency Words — Unit 2 ★

children	people	happy	of	onto

★ High Frequency Words — Unit 3 ★

so	over	asked	didn't	suddenly
morning	very	only	across	many

★ High Frequency Words — Unit 4 ★

live	middle	yesterday	any
again	don't	today	other

ANSWERS

Review and Assessment Sections

Please note that answers may vary slightly for some questions.

UNIT 1 - Spelling

Page 18	car, shorts, nurse, fern, corn, farm, bird, church
Page 19	1 star, barn, fern, skirt, horse, purse; 2 shirt, jar, shark, fern, ball, curl, bird, barn, four

Comprehension

Page 21	1b, 2d, 3b, 4a, 5 black, 6b, 7a, 8b, 9d, 10d 1 giraffe, 2 laugh, 3 horse, 4 bird, 5 barn farm, 6 corn, 7 shirt, 8 dirt, 9 stir

UNIT 2 - Spelling

Page 30	tear, clown, hare, cloud, coil, deer, boy, chair
Page 31	1 house, cow, point, bear, boy, pear; 2 bear, deer, sphere, owl, hair, pair

Comprehension

Page 33	1c, 2b, 3b, 4b, 5 crowd, 6c, 7b, 8a, 9c, 10 happy 1 howl, 2 flour, 3 boil, 4 buoys, 5 year, 6 steer, 7 pair, 8 pear share, 9 wear

UNIT 3 - Spelling

Page 42	hedge, stitch, screw, stripes, splash, spring, shrimp, throne
Page 43	1 three, bridge, stream, witch, shrub, throne; 2 bridge, splint, match, shrub, three, spray, splits, stream, screw

Comprehension

Page 45	1c, 2d, 3b, 4a, 5b, 6d, 7b, 8d, 9 The children put their bikes near a small shrub. 10 The rock falling into the water made the big splash. 1 hatch, 2 fridge, 3 scrub, 4 strong, 5 spread, 6 splash, 7 through

UNIT 4 - Spelling

Page 54	1 having, 2 throwing, 3 bouncing, 4 kicking, 5 playing, 6 turning, 7 jumping, 8 had, 9 threw, 10 bounced, 11 kicked, 12 played, 13 turned, 14 jumped
Page 55	Largest, large, larger. Light, lighter, lightest, youngest, younger, young. Tall, taller, tallest. Old, older, oldest.

Comprehension

Page 57	1a, 2c, 3b, 4c, 5c, 6b, 7b, 8d, 9 The smallest goat crossed the bridge first. 10 The bridge started breaking up when the goats crossed it. 1 better, 2 fastest, 3 played, 4 strongest, 5 helping, 6 dances, 7 having

  ISBN: 9781925726367

UNIT 5 - Spelling

Page 66	pea + nut 2 syllables; choc + o + late 3 syllables; gor + il + la 3 syllables; trum + pet 2 syllables; kan + gar + oo 3 syllables; dol + phin 2 syllables

Page 67	table: 1 syllable: shark, branch, cloud; 2 syllables: wombat, kitten, dragon, insect, playful, plastic, cupboard; 3 syllables: echidna, platypus, carpenter, animal, finishing, fantastic; 4 syllables: cauliflower, escalator, environment
	1 escalator, 2 kitten, 3 cauliflower, 4 platypus, 5 carpenter, 6 dragon, 7 environment, 8 fantastic

Comprehension

Page 69	1 Six species of sea turtles live in Australian waters. 2 All six species of Australian sea turtles are protected. 3 Rubbish is a hazard because if sea turtles swallow it they can die. 4 If rubbish is left lying around, it can get washed into waterways or blown into the ocean. 5 Fishing can hurt turtles if they get caught in the nets or tangled in the lines. 6 Watercraft can injure sea turtles by accidentally hitting them. 7 Watercraft include boats, ships, and jet skis. 8 Vehicles driving on the beach are a danger because they can destroy turtles' nests and eggs. 9 Baby turtles are called hatchlings. 10 You can help save sea turtles by picking up rubbish you see on the beach.
	Australian, endangered, protected, waterways, accidents, watercraft, vehicles, difficulty, visiting, organisations

UNIT 6 - Spelling

Page 78	comb, home, knot, ghost, sword, wreath, knife, bomb, gnat
Page 79	table: Silent 'h': wheat, honest, wheel, school; Silent 'w': wrist, wreck, wrong, write; Silent 'k': knot, kneel, knew, knock; Silent 'g': gnat, gnaw, sign, gnome; Silent 'b': comb, crumb, climb, doubt
	1 wrong, 2 knock, 3 wheat, 4 knew, 5 write, 6 school, 7 sign, 8 knot, 9 comb, 10 climb

Comprehension

Page 81	1 My story is about a boy who wants to be a knight. 2 The story takes place in the past. 3 I wouldn't give the knight a pretend sword as boys are unlikely to have knives. 4 The knight is brave and honest. 5 The knight's troops are a garden gnome and clay lamb brought to life. 6 The knight follows signs to get to the castle. 7 When the knight gets to the castle, he knocks on the door. 8 The knight's face will go white with fear if he sees a ghost. 9 and 10 personal responses will vary.
	write, who, when, where, what, why, knight, knife, sword, wrong, doubt, would, know, though, honest, gnome, lamb, climb, signs, knock, ghost, white, fright, knitting, answers

  ISBN: 9781925726367

UNIT 7 - Spelling

Page 90	treasure, collision, balloon, salad, baby, bubble, lotion, puddle, lady
Page 91	table: football, spaceship, superhero, dragonfly, backpack, cupcake, toolbox, spiderweb, hairbrush
	1 dragonfly, 2 spaceship, 3 cupcake, 4 hairbrush, 5 superhero, 6 spiderweb, 7 football, 8 backpack, 9 toolbox

Comprehension

Page 93	1 The story takes place in summer. 2 Jamie's family goes to the Beachside Vacation Park for the holidays. 3 Jamie is diving through waves and riding his bodyboard when he pretends to be a turtle or a dolphin. 4 Jamie finds starfish, whelks and crabs in the rockpools. 5 Jamie sees jellyfish and seaweed washed up on the shore. 6 Jamie and his friends are not allowed to go to the shipwreck. 7 The children are not allowed to go because the shipwreck is dangerous. 8 The children pretend the shipwreck is a pirate ship. 9 Jamie's friend is called Corey. 10 The man is not a real pirate because they do not exist in the modern day.
	beachside, summertime, bodyboards, starfish, sometimes, jellyfish, seaweed, seashore, shipwreck, footprints

ASSESSMENT - Spelling

Page 95	1 shorts, farm, church, cloud, chair, screw, throne, wreck, match, ghost, baby, knight; 2 curl, bear, bridge, splits, comb, sword, knife, balloon, house, giraffe, deer, boy
Page 96	1 laugh, 2 steer, 3 hatch, 4 strongest, 5 operation, 6 mayor, 7 badge, 8 pouch, 9 shrimp, 10 knock, 11 rode, 12 playing, 13 winner, 14 fixed, 15 talks, 16 taught, 17 running, 18 read, 19 watched, 20 going
Page 97	1 longest, long, longer; highest, high, higher; bright, brightest, brighter
	table 1 syllable: desk, mouse, cord; 2 syllables: keyboard, tablet, laptop, program, website, bandwidth; 3 syllables: computer, digital, processor, internet; 4 syllables: security, compatible

Comprehension

Page 99	1 People can use desktop computers as well as mobile devices like phones, tablets and laptops. 2 People can access the internet anywhere. 3 A mobile device can be easily moved while a desktop computer stays in the one place. 4 a People can write emails while on the internet; b People can look up information while on the internet. 5 Children learn how to use computers at school. 6 Children learn how to create and save files. 7 Children learn how to access the internet safely. 8 Children have to check that the website and information are reliable. 9 Before starting school, young children use the internet to play games and watch videos. 10 The internet is very important to modern life.
	everyone, internet, anywhere, laptops, desktop, workplace, anything, keyboard, trackpad, download, website

  ISBN: 9781925726367